TO

_____

FROM

_____

DATE

_____

100 DAYS OF

Hope & Encouragement

A DEVOTIONAL JOURNAL

DaySpring

LIVE YOUR FAITH

YOU HAVE A REASON FOR HOPE.

You are loved, you are special, you are known.
You are blessed, you are held, and you are forgiven.
You are important. You have a purpose.
You are guided, equipped and able.

YOU ARE NOT ALONE.

It can be hard to believe, hard to hold on to,
sometimes. But this is your true identity as a child of God.
It's our prayer that the devotions in this journal will gently
and faithfully remind you of who you are in Him.

May the God of hope fill you with all joy and peace
in believing, so that you may abound in hope. And may your
heart be encouraged — over the next 100 days and every day —
through the life-giving promises of God.

TRUE ROYALTY

You are created in the image of God, the much-beloved daughter of the King of heaven. And at the same time, you are the Bride of Christ, His Son, called to rule and reign with Him now and in eternity. (The Bible often compares the relationship between God and His people to a love story or a romance. Those who believe in Jesus are collectively described as His "Bride.") So every way you look at it, you're true royalty! You are chosen. You are loved and cherished. The King delights in your beauty. Don't ever forget it. Let this powerful truth fill your heart with confidence and joy today—and with a deep, deep love for the One who first loved you and gave Himself for you.

He has rescued us from the kingdom of darkness and
transferred us into the Kingdom of His dear Son.
COLOSSIANS 1:13 NLT

Now listen, daughter, don't miss a word: forget your country,
put your home behind you. Be here—*the King is wild for you.*
Since He's your Lord, adore Him.
PSALM 45:10—11 THE MESSAGE

He forgives your sins—every one. He heals your diseases—every one.
He redeems you from hell—saves your life! He crowns you with love and
mercy—a paradise crown. He wraps you in goodness—beauty eternal.
He renews your youth—you're always young in His presence.
PSALM 103:3—5 THE MESSAGE

Consider the kind of extravagant love the Father has lavished on us—
He calls us children of God! It's true; we are His beloved children.

I JOHN 3:1 VOICE

"Beloved", extravagant, wrapped in goodness is difficult to picture. Yet that is my reality. Help me to see, experience, walk in, wake in the promise of who you say I am. Like my own children — oh god, I love them so, so much. I cannot fathom that you love me more.

Help me too, to see you in the awe and splendor you deserve. Worshipful wonder. Fear and holiness. The train of your robe fills the temple — may I see that in my heart? God I trust that the words that have existed for generation to generation ~~ring~~ ring true, and I trust they will reign in my heart for me to fully know you, love you. Adore you

Lord, Your love has captured my heart. I am Yours,

now and for always. How I love You! With all that I am,

I worship and adore You.

SOMETHING SPECIAL

God has always had a plan and a purpose for you. Before you were even born, He knew how He would create you, all the gifts and talents He would give you, and all the ways He would work in and through you. He knew what life experiences would best prepare you. It may not always be clear to you what His purpose is or how He is bringing it all together, but He is. Your challenge is to give it some thought, some prayer, some reflection—but not to get too caught up in trying to figure it all out. Just do the best you can with what you have, with what He's given you. Develop those gifts and talents. Find practical or creative ways to use them. Look for His direction and say yes to wherever He calls you.

Remember to use the gift that you have.
I TIMOTHY 4:14 ICB

Concentrate on doing your best for God.
II TIMOTHY 2:15 THE MESSAGE

God who began the good work within you will keep right on helping you grow in His grace until His task within you is finally finished on that day when Jesus Christ returns.
PHILIPPIANS 1:6 TLB

It is clear to us, friends, that God not only loves you very much but also has put His hand on you for something special.

I THESSALONIANS 1:4 THE MESSAGE

_____

_____

_____

_____

_____

_____

_____

_____

_____

_____

_____

_____

_____

_____

God, help me to receive with thanksgiving the gifts You've given me. Help me to make the best of them, to use them to fulfill Your plans and purposes, Your calling.

SOMETHING BEAUTIFUL

Sometimes we feel like a hot mess. We try so hard to hide our faults and flaws and imperfections. We're embarrassed and ashamed of all the ways we can't seem to measure up. And there are plenty of voices to tell us that whatever we are, it's not enough. But not the voice of Jesus. Over and over in Scripture, He tells us that He knows all about it; He knows all about us. And He loves us. Oh, how He loves us! He promises that He will help us. He will get in there with us, in the middle of the mess, and, by His power and grace, make something beautiful out of it. He will make something beautiful out of us.

So I am well pleased with weakness, with insults, with distresses, with persecutions, and with difficulties, for the sake of Christ, for when I am weak [in human strength], then I am strong [truly able, truly powerful, truly drawing from God's strength].

II CORINTHIANS 12:10 AMP

In the same way the Spirit [comes to us and] helps us in our weakness. We do not know what prayer to offer or how to offer it as we should, but the Spirit Himself [knows our need and at the right time] intercedes on our behalf.

ROMANS 8:26 AMP

My grace is all you need. My power works best in weakness.

II CORINTHIANS 12:9 NLT

Jesus, I know I'm sometimes a hot mess, but I'm Your hot mess. Help me to be something more today, someone who loves You and trusts You and rests in Your grace.

SMALL BEGINNINGS

Sometimes our best efforts seem so small. Nothing we do feels like it's "enough." We don't seem to have much influence or impact. We don't know how we can make a difference, bring about change, accomplish an important task, or achieve anything significant. But God says not to "despise" or look down on small beginnings. From the tiniest seeds grow the biggest trees. And God will help us. He will give us strength. He will give us wisdom and direction. He will bless even our smallest efforts, our tiniest steps—beyond anything we can imagine—when we're faithful to do what He's asked us. Don't get discouraged. Don't give up or give in. The best is yet to come! This is only the beginning.

So let's not get tired of doing what is good. At just the right time we will reap a harvest of blessing if we don't give up.

GALATIANS 6:9 NLT

Come and see what our God has done, what awesome miracles He performs for people!

PSALM 66:5 NLT

Let us know and become personally acquainted with Him; let us press on to know and understand fully the [greatness of the] LORD [to honor, heed, and deeply cherish Him]. His appearing is prepared and is as certain as the dawn, and He will come to us [in salvation] like the [heavy] rain, like the spring rain watering the earth.

HOSEA 6:3 AMP

Do not despise these small beginnings,
for the LORD rejoices to see the work begin.

ZECHARIAH 4:10 NLT

Lord, give me the courage to keep on keeping on!

Help me to trust that small steps will lead to big ones...

and that You will show up. Help me to be patient in the process.

CONVERSATION STARTER

It's kind of staggering, really. In this Scripture, God invites us to sit down and have a conversation with Him about our sin. He knows all about the selfishness, the complacency, the words we spoke in anger, the grumbling and complaining. Our hearts are covered in stains, weighed down by guilt and shame. It's a problem, all right. And there's nothing we can do to solve it. We have nothing to bargain with, nothing we can bring to the table.

But God, in His great mercy and love, offers us the deal of the centuries: His Son Jesus will pay the price and take the penalty in our place. He will cover for us. More than that, He will cleanse us: scrub our heart fresh and clean and forgive us through and through. All we have to do is receive this incredible gift. Receive His forgiveness. As often as we come to Him, as often as we ask, He will make us new.

I confess my sins; I am deeply sorry for what I have done.

PSALM 38:18 NLT

Have mercy on me, O God, because of Your unfailing love.
Because of Your great compassion, blot out the stain of my sins.

PSALM 51:1 NLT

Create pure thoughts in me and make me faithful again.

PSALM 51:10 CEV

Come now, let us reason together, says the LORD:
though your sins are like scarlet, they shall be white as snow.

ISAIAH 1:18 ESV

Jesus, I can't thank You enough for what You have done for me.

I'm so grateful to You. I receive Your love, Your mercy,

Your grace—and I rest in Your embrace.

A WILLING HEART

For centuries, scholars, theologians, artists, musicians, and poets have wondered: What was so special about the girl from Nazareth, a young woman called Mary? Why did God choose her, above all the other women on earth, to be the mother of His Son? Was it the purity of her heart or the depth of her devotion to Him? Did she have the perfect personality or was she a beauty beyond compare? What made her stand out?

The Gospel of Luke gives us a clue: it's the way she responds to the angel's message. She asks a natural question, "How can this be?" But then she doesn't argue or deliberate. She doesn't insist on having all the details ahead of time. She doesn't grumble or complain. She believes. And she says "Yes!" She will be whatever God wants her to be and do whatever God asks her to do. What made Mary special? What made her a woman God could use? She had a willing heart. We can have one too.

Behold, I am the servant of the Lord;
may it be done to me according to Your word.
LUKE 1:38 AMP

The Mighty One has done great things for me; holy is God's name!
LUKE 1:49 VOICE

Blessed is she who has believed that the Lord
would fulfill His promises to her!
LUKE 1:45 NIV

Oh, how my soul praises the Lord.
How my spirit rejoices in God my Savior!

LUKE 1:46–47 NLT

_____
_____
_____
_____
_____
_____
_____
_____
_____
_____
_____
_____
_____
_____

God, I, too, believe. I, too, am willing—at least I'm willing to be made willing—to be whatever You ask me to be and to do whatever You ask me to do, out of love for You.

FASHIONED BY DESIGN

You are not an accident or a mistake. There is nothing about you that is generic or derivative or "mass-produced." No, you are a true masterpiece, unique and one-of-a-kind, fashioned by design. Beautifully handcrafted by God Himself. Every detail is exquisite, purposeful, and deliberate. Your personality and temperament, background and life experiences, gifts and talents—all these things make you, you. All these things make you—and you alone—perfect for the plan God has for you. Embrace this truth! Celebrate your true beauty, a reflection of your Creator's beauty. Use it to help others discover His beauty—and their own.

It's in Christ that we find out who we are and what we are living for. Long before we first heard of Christ and got our hopes up, He had His eye on us, had designs on us for glorious living, part of the overall purpose He is working out in everything and everyone.

EPHESIANS 1:11–12 THE MESSAGE

We have a special role in His plan. He calls us to life by His message of truth so that we will show the rest of His creatures His goodness and love.

JAMES 1:18 VOICE

You are a chosen people. You are royal priests, a holy nation, God's very own possession. As a result, you can show others the goodness of God, for He called you out of the darkness into His wonderful light.

I PETER 2:9 NLT

God saved us and called us to live a holy life. He did this, not because we deserved it, but because that was His plan from before the beginning of time—to show us His grace through Christ Jesus.

II TIMOTHY 1:9 NLT

Glorious God, help me to reflect Your light, reveal Your truth, and radiate Your goodness and love, that others may be deeply drawn to You.

GOD'S INSCRIPTION

When you were a child, did your parents ever accidentally leave you at a mall or a restaurant? Was there a time when each thought the other had picked you up from school? Were you ever left off the invitation list to a special party? Ignored or overlooked by others at church or at work? At one time or another, we've all experienced the pain of feeling abandoned, rejected, neglected, or unloved. The Bible describes a time when God's people felt that way. They thought that He had forgotten and forsaken them. But God said, "No way!"

He will never, ever let go of His people. He will never leave us or forsake us. In fact, He loves us so much that He has our names "inscribed" or "engraved" on the palms of His hands, where He will always see them and be reminded of how much we mean to Him. Those same hands are holding our hearts and lives today.

I entrust my spirit into Your hands. You have redeemed me,
O Eternal, God of faithfulness and truth.
PSALM 31:5 VOICE

Even if my father and mother abandon me,
the Lord will hold me close.
PSALM 27:10 NLT

My future is in Your hands.
PSALM 31:15 NLT

I, God, will never forget you. Look here. I have made you a part of Me,
written you on the palms of My hands.

ISAIAH 49:15–16 VOICE

Father, thank You for holding me so close and loving me so

dearly. No matter where I go or what happens to me,

I know that I am safe in Your hands.

MORE THAN ENOUGH

We live in a world that actively encourages a "scarcity mindset," a deep and driving belief that whatever we need, there won't be enough. We have to grab whatever we can get—right now, this very minute—even if it's not exactly what we want or need. And we hold on to it (or hoard it) for dear life. Because we just don't know if anything more or anything else will ever be available to us. We end up turning our lives into one big, anxious, scary scavenger hunt, desperately spending all our time and energy in trying to provide for ourselves and get our needs met. But God says it's His job to provide for us. He promises that He will equip us for every challenge we face. He will meet every need. And His resources aren't at all scarce. In fact, they're lavish, abundant, and overflowing. So much more than enough.

Open your mouth wide, and I will fill it with good things.

PSALM 81:10 NLT

Know this: my God will also fill every need you have according to His glorious riches in Jesus the Anointed, our Liberating King.

PHILIPPIANS 4:19 VOICE

Steep yourself in God-reality, God-initiative, God-provisions. You'll find all your everyday human concerns will be met. Don't be afraid of missing out.... The Father wants to give you the very kingdom itself.

LUKE 12:31–32 THE MESSAGE

Give us each day our daily bread.

LUKE 11:3 AMP

Lord Jesus, help me to see all the ways You are providing for me and meeting my needs. Help me to trust You to be more than enough for me.

BEING YOU

The beauty of creation is nothing compared to the beauty God sees in you! You are so precious to Him, so valuable, so important. Not because of any earthly power or significance or influence you have and not because of anything you have done or will do. Not because of what you can give or "contribute." Not because of anything you can earn or accomplish or achieve. No, you don't have to do a thing. You are beautiful and precious and valuable and important to God because you are you. Because He loves you. Because He created you. You are specially designed, unique, and one-of-a-kind. It's more than enough—you are more than enough—just being you.

Look at the birds in the sky. They do not store food for winter. They don't plant gardens. They do not sow or reap—and yet, they are always fed because your heavenly Father feeds them. And you are even more precious to Him than a beautiful bird. If He looks after them, of course He will look after you.

MATTHEW 6:26 VOICE

Since you are so much more precious to God than a thousand flocks of sparrows, and since God knows you in every detail—down to the number of hairs on your head at this moment—you can be secure and unafraid of any person, and you have nothing to fear from God either.

LUKE 12:7 VOICE

Look at the lilies and how they grow. They don't work or make their clothing,
yet Solomon in all his glory was not dressed as beautifully as they are.

LUKE 12:27 NLT

Lord, help me to believe and trust in the love
You have for me. Help me to rest in that love.
Let my life bring joy and glory to You.

BATTLE TO VICTORY

The book of Judges tells the story of a woman who chose not to sit on the sidelines— or, in this case, under a palm tree—when a national crisis called for action. Deborah, a prophetess, was leading Israel at that time. She held court under the Palm of Deborah, in the hill country, and the people came to her to settle their disputes. God guided her and gifted her with supernatural wisdom and spiritual discernment. And on a day when the courage of men failed, Deborah led the armies of Israel into battle against the enemies that had so long attacked and harassed and oppressed them. She put the plan God had given her into action and God was true to His Word: He gave His people the victory.

He promises to guide us the same way, to give us the wisdom we need not only for ordinary, everyday challenges but also for the biggest battles we face. When we follow His lead, as Deborah did, we'll find ourselves singing His praises and celebrating our victory!

Listen, you kings! Pay attention, you mighty rulers! For I will sing to the Lord. I will make music to the Lord, the God of Israel.

JUDGES 5:3 NLT

Yours, O Lord, is the greatness, the power, the glory, the victory, and the majesty.

I CHRONICLES 29:11 NLT

Yes, You are my rock and my fortress; for Your Name's sake You will lead me and guide me.

PSALM 31:3 AMP

I praise You, LORD! You are my mighty rock,
and You teach me how to fight my battles.

PSALM 144:1 CEV

Thank You, God, for teaching me and leading me and guiding me. Thank You for teaching me to fight. Thank You for each and every victory!

HOLDING ONTO HOPE

Maybe you've heard the expression, "Everything will be all right in the end. If it's not all right, it's not the end!" This little proverb is not in the Bible, but it could be. It captures the essence of dozens of verses that remind us to be patient and wait in hope as God continues His work in the world. We're a little out of practice (not just patience). So many things in our lives are now immediate and instantaneous. We find it really, really hard to wait. Yet so many of the best things—the richest and deepest and most complex, the brightest and most beautiful, the most rewarding and satisfying—still take time. Especially stories. Our stories, God's story. We may not be able to see it yet. We can't figure out how it all fits together or how it could possibly turn out for the best. But God says it does—it will. Hang in there. Hold on. Have hope.

> We can rejoice, too, when we run into problems and trials, for we know
> that they help us develop endurance. And endurance develops strength
> of character, and character strengthens our confident hope of salvation.
> And this hope will not lead to disappointment. For we know how dearly
> God loves us.
>
> ROMANS 5:3–5 NLT

> So let's do it—full of belief, confident that we're presentable inside and
> out. Let's keep a firm grip on the promises that keep us going. He always
> keeps His word.
>
> HEBREWS 10:22–23 THE MESSAGE

> The Lord is good to those who put their hope in Him.
> He is good to those who look to Him for help.
>
> LAMENTATIONS 3:25 ICB

Now the Lord is not slow about enacting His promise—slow is how some people want to characterize it—no, He is not slow but patient.

II PETER 3:9 VOICE

_____
_____
_____
_____
_____
_____
_____
_____
_____
_____
_____
_____
_____

God, help me to hold on to hope. Help me to not give up or lose heart or walk out and miss the gloriously happy ending You have in store. I'm trusting in You.

WHAT IS LOVE?

Sometimes we wonder if we really know what love is. We've seen so many twisted, mixed-up, messed-up versions of it. Does love even exist? Truly? God says He sent His Son Jesus to show us, to help us see what it means to be loved for real, perfectly, deeply, and truly. That's how Jesus loves. He loved us so much that He was willing to die for us, to give up His own life to save us. He lived a life of love to set us an example—not only of how He loves us but how we, with His help, can love others. Thanks to Jesus, we really do know what love is.

This is real love—not that we loved God, but that He loved us and sent His Son as a sacrifice to take away our sins.

I JOHN 4:10 NLT

Love is patient and kind. Love is not jealous or boastful or proud or rude. It does not demand its own way. It is not irritable, and it keeps no record of being wronged. It does not rejoice about injustice but rejoices whenever the truth wins out. Love never gives up, never loses faith, is always hopeful, and endures through every circumstance.

I CORINTHIANS 13:4—7 NLT

Three things will last forever—faith, hope, and love— and the greatest of these is love.

I CORINTHIANS 13:13 NLT

For God so loved the world that He gave His one and only Son,
that whoever believes in Him shall not perish but have eternal life.

JOHN 3:16 NIV

Dear Jesus, thank You for loving me.

Thank You for dying on the cross to show me—to save me

and to set me free for all eternity. How I love You!

ALONG THE ROAD

When Jesus was crucified, His friends were overcome by shock, grief, and despair. He had told them that it was going to happen, but they didn't understand. They had put all their hope and faith in Him—and now He was gone. They felt abandoned and alone. Two of them left Jerusalem, heading for Emmaus. A Stranger joined them along the road. He listened to them pour out their hearts, and then He spoke. Into their darkness, He spoke light and life and truth. He challenged them to see with new eyes, to hear with new ears, to view the circumstances from God's perspective. And suddenly they saw Him. They realized that the Stranger was Jesus Himself—risen from the dead, just as He had said. He had kept His promise. He had not abandoned them. He would never abandon them. They were not alone. And neither are we.

Be strong and courageous. Do not be afraid; do not be discouraged, for the LORD your God will be with you wherever you go.

JOSHUA 1:9 NIV

Be sure of this—that I am with you always, even to the end of the world.

MATTHEW 28:20 TLB

I will never leave you; I will always be by your side.

HEBREWS 13:5 VOICE

They said to each other, "Didn't our hearts burn within us as He talked with us on the road and explained the Scriptures to us?"

LUKE 24:32 NLT

_____

_____

_____

_____

_____

_____

_____

_____

_____

_____

_____

_____

_____

_____

Lord Jesus, please be with me today. Keep me company on this journey. Hear my heart and help me to find comfort, courage, and strength in You.

KNOWN BY NAME

Shakespeare asked, "What's in a name?" Through the character of Juliet, he was, of course, musing whether two young lovers from rival families should let their family names keep them apart. Does it matter what something or someone is called?

In the Bible, God says He has made all of us a part of one family—His family. And even though He has many, many, many children, our heavenly Father knows each and every one by name. He never accidentally calls us by a brother's or sister's name. He never gets us confused with anyone else. He knows exactly who we are. He knows and loves us—deeply, personally, intimately, individually.

Before I shaped you in the womb, I knew all about you. Before you saw the light of day, I had holy plans for you.

JEREMIAH 1:5 THE MESSAGE

Fear not, for I have redeemed you; I have called you by name, you are mine.

ISAIAH 43:1 ESV

I am pleased with you and I know you by name.

EXODUS 33:17 NIV

God doesn't count us; He calls us by name.

ROMANS 9:27 THE MESSAGE

Father, I'm so glad I belong to You, that You know me and love me the way You do. Help me to live in the light of this glorious truth, for the glory and honor of Your name.

LAST AND LEAST

When Samuel announced that God had sent him to anoint Israel's next king, Jesse proudly produced all eight of his strapping sons, eager to see which God would choose. Well, seven. David was the eighth, the last and the least, and his own family completely forgot about him. No one bothered to call him in from the fields, where he was watching the sheep. They didn't think it was important; they didn't think he was important. But as God said no to brother after brother, it soon became clear: David was His choice.

Over and over in Scripture, God reminds us that He has a different standard, a different way of measuring things. And that there are no limits to what He can do. A heart like David's—a heart that fully belongs to Him—that's the most important thing. So God called David from the pasture to the palace, to rule as Israel's greatest king. And He made him part of Jesus's family tree. Imagine what He can do with you!

The LORD doesn't see things the way you see them. People judge by
outward appearance, but the LORD looks at the heart.
I SAMUEL 16:7 NLT

Do not despise these small beginnings,
for the LORD rejoices to see the work begin.
ZECHARIAH 4:10 NLT

Well done, my good and faithful servant. You have been faithful
in handling this small amount, so now I will give you many more
responsibilities. Let's celebrate together!
MATTHEW 25:23 NLT

The LORD says, "Bethlehem Ephrathah, you are one of the smallest towns in Judah, but out of you I will bring a ruler for Israel, whose family line goes back to ancient times."

MICAH 5:2 GNT

Lord, help me to love You with my whole heart as David did and to be faithful in everything You ask me to do, big or small, for Your kingdom and Your glory.

IF WE FORGIVE

It's not easy to forgive the wounds others have inflicted on us, whether minor or major, careless, thoughtless, or cruelly deliberate. But God calls us to do it. He calls us to choose to let go of the anger and resentment. Choose to give others the benefit of the doubt. Seek to understand. Show compassion, patience, kindness. Extend mercy and grace—even when they don't deserve it. Because we don't deserve it, and yet that's exactly how God responds to us.

Yes, we may have to set some healthy boundaries. No, it's not always possible for the relationship to be fully reconciled, especially if the other person is no longer living or is unrepentant and/or unsafe. But still we forgive—as an act of obedience and gratitude to God for all that He has forgiven us. We forgive so that no one else (including ourselves) will be poisoned by the bitterness of unforgiveness. Healing takes place, if only in our own heart. And sometimes we will see all kinds of miracles of mercy and grace.

In prayer there is a connection between what God does and what you do. You can't get forgiveness from God, for instance, without also forgiving others. If you refuse to do your part, you cut yourself off from God's part.
MATTHEW 6:14–15 THE MESSAGE

Be kind and helpful to one another, tender-hearted [compassionate, understanding], forgiving one another [readily and freely], just as God in Christ also forgave you.
EPHESIANS 4:32 AMP

Forgive us the wrongs we have done,
as we forgive the wrongs that others have done to us.

MATTHEW 6:12 GNT

Lord Jesus, please heal my hurting heart and
help me to forgive others as You have so generously
and graciously forgiven me.

SET APART

The Bible sometimes uses the words "sanctified" and "holy" to mean "set apart," chosen by God for a special purpose. And that's exactly what you are! You may not always feel all that "holy" or special, but you are. God sent Jesus to make it so. He wanted you to know: you have been loved by God, chosen by God to belong to Him. You are "His people"—His family. He wants you to know Him and love Him the way He knows and loves you ... and to live in a way that reflects His love, in a way that invites others to come to know and love Him too.

The LORD has chosen everyone who is faithful to be His very own.

PSALM 4:3 CEV

You were washed [by the atoning sacrifice of Christ], you were sanctified [set apart for God, and made holy], you were justified [declared free of guilt] in the name of the Lord Jesus Christ and in the [Holy] Spirit of our God [the source of the believer's new life and changed behavior].

I CORINTHIANS 6:11 AMP

For God's will was for us to be made holy by the sacrifice of the body of Jesus Christ, once for all time.

HEBREWS 10:10 NLT

God loves you and has chosen you as His own special people.

COLOSSIANS 3:12 CEV

God, thank You for choosing me, for setting me apart, for making me whole and holy in You. Help me to shine with Your love and Your light, bringing glory and honor to You.

A KING'S RESCUE

Once upon a time, we were held captive by our doubts, our fears, our anger and frustrations, our insecurities, and our obsessions. We were enslaved by sin, selfishness, and self-absorption. Our many attempts to free ourselves and escape only ended in failure and defeat. Feeling hopeless, we gave up—and gave in to despair.

But suddenly the King appeared. He came to rescue us and set us free. He threw open the doors of our dark dungeon and let in the Light. He paid the penalty for our sin and declared us "not guilty." He invited us to rule and reign with Him in His eternal kingdom.

And now we are free. Free to live, free to love, free to serve Him willingly and faithfully and, yes, happily ever after.

Lift up your heads, O gates, and lift them up, ancient doors,
that the King of glory may come in.

PSALM 24:9 AMP

Those who have been rescued will go up to Mount Zion...
and the LORD Himself will be King.

OBADIAH 1:21 NLT

I broke the yoke of slavery from your neck so you can walk
with your heads held high.

LEVITICUS 26:13 NLT

Christ has set us free to live a free life. So take your stand!
Never again let anyone put a harness of slavery on you.

GALATIANS 5:1 THE MESSAGE

Jesus, You are my hero! A mighty Savior, the King of kings!

Thank You for rescuing me. Help me to live a life brave and free

and fulfill Your plans and purposes for me.

EVERLASTING ARMS

His arms never get tired. His love never grows cold. He never lets go of you or gives up on you or gets over you. God's love for you is everlasting. So are His arms, which hold you tight. The arms that support you and strengthen you, cradle you and comfort you—the arms that catch you when you fall. You don't have to be afraid of anything, now or ever. God is eternal and forever. He is faithful. He will be with you; He will carry you through it all. Rest in Him. Rest in His everlasting love; rest in His everlasting arms today.

The Eternal God is your shelter;
He holds you up in His everlasting arms.
DEUTERONOMY 33:27 VOICE

Those the LORD has rescued will return. They will enter Zion with singing; everlasting joy will crown their heads. Gladness and joy will overtake them, and sorrow and sighing will flee away.
ISAIAH 51:11 NIV

Your kingdom is an everlasting kingdom. You rule throughout all generations. The LORD always keeps His promises; He is gracious in all He does.
PSALM 145:13 NLT

I have loved you, My people, with an everlasting love.
With unfailing love I have drawn you to Myself.

JEREMIAH 31:3 NLT

God, thank You for loving me, for caring for me, for carrying me.

Help me to rest, to be still, to relax, and to trust You.

You hold me safe in Your everlasting arms.

GIFTS THAT KEEP GIVING

You are incredibly gifted! God has blessed you with all kinds of natural talents, abilities, and skills, plus a wealth of wisdom, knowledge, and life experience. The Bible says He's also blessed you with "spiritual gifts," supernatural gifts that empower you to live out your high and holy calling, gifts that enable you to be a blessing to others. Gifts that are desperately needed in the Body of Christ—God's family of believers—so that we can be strong and healthy and function properly. If it's been a while, take some time to make a list of your gifts, thank God for them, and think of ways you can give them (or "regift" them) to others.

Some of us have been given special ability as apostles; to others He has given the gift of being able to preach well; some have special ability in winning people to Christ, helping them to trust Him as their Savior; still others have a gift for caring for God's people as a shepherd does his sheep, leading and teaching them in the ways of God.

EPHESIANS 4:11 TLB

There are different kinds of gifts; but they are all from the same Spirit. There are different ways to serve; but all these ways are from the same Lord. And there are different ways that God works in people; but all these ways are from the same God. God works in us all in everything we do.

I CORINTHIANS 12:4—6 ICB

Each of you has been blessed with one of God's many wonderful gifts to be used in the service of others. So use your gift well.

I PETER 4:10 CEV

Jesus, thank You for each of the precious gifts You have given me. Help me to use them well, for the benefit of others and for Your kingdom and Your glory.

LOST AND FOUND

There's a beautiful, glorious gift that comes to us in the midst of our ugliest, most excruciating suffering and pain: a deeper intimacy with God, a stronger sensitivity to His presence, a greater awareness of His power at work in us. And a dramatic shift in our perspective and priorities. As Holocaust survivor Corrie ten Boom once said, "You never know Jesus is all you need until Jesus is all you have." Through their grief and pain and loss, Corrie and countless others testify to this powerful truth: "There is no pit so deep that God's love is not deeper still."

None of us want to learn this the hard way, but sometimes the hard way seems to be the only way. And it's worth it. It's worth losing all we have to find all we need in Him.

Just as Christ's sufferings are ours in abundance [as they overflow to His followers], so also our comfort [our reassurance, our encouragement, our consolation] is abundant through Christ [it is truly more than enough to endure what we must].

II CORINTHIANS 1:5 AMP

Even when I walk through the darkest valley, I will not be afraid, for You are close beside me.

PSALM 23:4 NLT

My comfort in my suffering is this: Your promise preserves my life.

PSALM 119:50 NIV

You're blessed when you feel you've lost what is most dear to you.
Only then can you be embraced by the One most dear to you.

MATTHEW 5:4 THE MESSAGE

Lord Jesus, draw me close to You. Hold me in my grief and pain. Comfort me in my loss with Your great love. Lift my gaze. Let me see Your face.

VICTORIOUS IN HIM

You don't have to keep making the same mistakes. You don't have to keep falling and failing, giving into temptation and sin. You can resist temptation. You can refuse poor choices. You can escape unhealthy patterns and behaviors. You can stand strong in Jesus.

Ask Him to help you, and He will! Ask Him to protect you. Ask Him to lead you and guide you. He will! Because He loves you, Jesus will steady you when you stumble, forgive you when you fall, and give you the courage and grace to get back up and try again. He'll show you how to break free from the past. He'll show you how to avoid the traps, pitfalls, and dangers ahead. You can be victorious in Him today.

And lead us not into temptation, but deliver us from evil.

MATTHEW 6:13 ESV

No temptation [regardless of its source] has overtaken or enticed you
that is not common to human experience [nor is any temptation
unusual or beyond human resistance]; but God is faithful [to His
word—He is compassionate and trustworthy], and He will not let you
be tempted beyond your ability [to resist], but along with the temptation
He [has in the past and is now and] will [always] provide the way out
as well, so that you will be able to endure it [without yielding, and will
overcome temptation with joy].

I CORINTHIANS 10:13 AMP

Since He Himself has now been through suffering and temptation,
He knows what it is like when we suffer and are tempted, and He is
wonderfully able to help us.

HEBREWS 2:18 TLB

He said to them, "Pray continually that you may not fall into temptation."

LUKE 22:40 AMP

Jesus, remind me to look for You in my trials and temptations:

look for Your help, look for Your strength, look for Your way of

escape. And help me to take it!

A SONG OF HOPE

Billy Graham said, "Let us be faithful in proclaiming the hope that is in Jesus. Sometimes hope feels elusive, ethereal, or small. But no matter how small, even a tiny bit of hope is powerful and persistent. Even when we think we don't want it, even when we dismiss it or despair of it, it sings to us, reminding us that wherever we are, whatever we're going through, no matter how hard or how dark it seems, all is not lost. This is not the end. And we are not alone. We have a mighty Savior who promises that He will fight for us, protect us, and defend us. He Himself will bring us through the stormy night to the dawn of a glorious new day.

He will cover you with His feathers. He will shelter you with His wings.
His faithful promises are your armor and protection.

PSALM 91:4 NLT

GOD is my strength, GOD is my song, and yes! GOD is my salvation.

EXODUS 15:2 THE MESSAGE

I will sing to the LORD because He is good to me.

PSALM 13:6 NLT

Why am I discouraged? Why is my heart so sad? I will put my hope in God!
I will praise Him again—my Savior and my God!

PSALM 42:11 NLT

Lord, fill my heart with hope today.
Help me to sing in the midst of the storm, with courage
and the confidence that You will see me through.

THE SHEPHERD'S LOVE

In the Bible, Jesus called Himself "the Good Shepherd": one willing to do anything for the sake of His "sheep." And He was—He did. He is. When danger comes, Jesus doesn't run off and leave us to our own defenses. No, He does everything in His power to protect us. He cares for us so tenderly, so lovingly. He leads us so gently and patiently. When we get lost or wander off, He comes after us. He seeks and saves us. When we struggle or stumble, He helps us. When life wounds us, He heals us. He restores our souls. What a joy to belong to such a Good Shepherd, to be His flock, the sheep of His pasture!

Know this: the Eternal One Himself is the True God. He is the One who made us; we have not made ourselves; we are His people, like sheep grazing in His fields.

PSALM 100:3 VOICE

He will feed His flock like a shepherd. He will carry the lambs in His arms, holding them close to His heart.

ISAIAH 40:11 NLT

He is our God and we are His people, the flock of His pasture, His sheep protected and nurtured by His hand.

PSALM 95:7 VOICE

The Good Shepherd lays down His [own] life for the sheep.

JOHN 10:11 AMP

_____

_____

_____

_____

_____

_____

_____

_____

_____

_____

_____

_____

_____

Good Shepherd, help me to be a good sheep! Help me to live in Your love, listen for Your voice, and follow where You lead.

STORMY WEATHER

It's hard to stay calm when the wind roars and the waves rage. It's hard to find rest and peace in the middle of a storm. But you are not alone. You don't face any of this alone. Jesus is with you. He will watch over you and protect you. He will comfort you and strengthen you. He has the power to speak to any storm and still it in an instant. And in the right instant (at the right moment), He will. Until then, try not to look at the wind whipping and the waves crashing or get all worried and worked up over things you can't control. Instead, look at Him. Keep your eyes on Jesus. He has everything under His control, including your current storm. Let Him be your refuge, your shelter, and He will fill you with perfect peace.

Mightier than the thunders of many waters, mightier than
the waves of the sea, the LORD on high is mighty!
PSALM 93:4 ESV

Peace be with you.
III JOHN 1:15 NLT

I have told you these things, so that in Me you may have [perfect]
peace. In the world you have tribulation and distress and suffering, but
be courageous [be confident, be undaunted, be filled with joy];
I have overcome the world. [My conquest is accomplished,
My victory abiding.]
JOHN 16:33 AMP

Jesus stood up and commanded the wind, "Be quiet!" and He said to the waves, "Be still!" The wind died down, and there was a great calm.

MARK 4:39 GNT

Jesus, speak to the storms in my life today—

calm "the wind and the waves" —and calm me.

Help me to hold onto Your peace.

ALWAYS ON HIS MIND

God is so crazy-in-love with you! He can't stop thinking about you. And He knows you better than anyone—better than you know yourself. He loves you so passionately, so deeply, so completely. You are always in His heart and on His mind.

You know what isn't on His mind? All your faults and failures, the things that fill you with guilt and shame and regret. Of course He knows about those things—He knows everything!—but they don't in any way diminish His love for you. Not even a little bit. He's covered them all with His forgiveness, mercy, and grace. Now all He wants to do is celebrate!

Even though our inner thoughts may condemn us with storms of guilt
and constant reminders of our failures, we can know in our hearts that
in His presence God Himself is greater than any accusation.
He knows all things.

I JOHN 3:20 VOICE

The Lord your God is in your midst,
a Warrior who saves.
He will rejoice over you with joy;
He will be quiet in His love [making no mention of your past sins],
He will rejoice over you with shouts of joy.

ZEPHANIAH 3:17 AMP

He is so good! His faithful love ... endures forever.

EZRA 3:11 NLT

"How precious are Your thoughts about me, O God.
They cannot be numbered!"

PSALM 139:17 NLT

God, it's hard for me to fully comprehend how well You know me and how much You love me. But I'm so glad You do. Help me to know You and love You that way too.

SHINING BRIGHTLY

Did you know that the encouragement to "shine" or "sparkle" isn't just a cheerful affirmation on a cute coffee mug or planner sticker or Facebook meme? It's actually an important part of your high and holy calling! When you shine with the light of God's love, you draw others to Him. When you sparkle with hope and faith and trust, when you tackle life's challenges with confidence and courage, you show others what Christ can do in you and through you. When, by God's grace, you choose to live a life of integrity, you set an inspiring example that invites others to do the same. So by all means, shine and glitter and sparkle with all that's in you—with Jesus, who is in you. Shine brightly!

Make your light shine, so that others will see the good that you do and will praise your Father in heaven.

MATTHEW 5:16 CEV

Do everything without complaining or arguing, so that you may be innocent and pure as God's perfect children, who live in a world of corrupt and sinful people. You must shine among them like stars lighting up the sky, as you offer them the message of life.

PHILIPPIANS 2:14–16 GNT

And those who are wise—the people of God—shall shine as brightly as the sun's brilliance, and those who turn many to righteousness will glitter like stars forever.

DANIEL 12:3 TLB

The righteous [those who seek the will of God] will shine forth [radiating the new life] like the sun in the kingdom of their Father.

MATTHEW 13:43 AMP

Lord Jesus, let my life bring Your light to a lost and dying world. Help me to be a beautiful reflection of Your love, mercy, and grace.

FORGIVEN LOVE

Her own community described her as a "sinful woman"—when they were speaking politely. On other occasions, they had lots of not-so-nice things to say about her life choices and her well-known faults and failures. There were many places a "woman of her kind" simply wasn't welcome.

But Jesus welcomed her. Jesus loved her. Jesus forgave her, fully and freely. Completely. In her gratitude, she couldn't speak. She could only weep—and let her tears wash His feet. Witnesses thought it was one more example of her inappropriate behavior. But Jesus received her expression—in all its emotion— as the gift that it was. A gift of love from a grateful heart.

Oh, what joy for those whose disobedience is forgiven,
whose sins are put out of sight.
ROMANS 4:7 NLT

As far as the east is from the west, so far has He removed
our transgressions from us.
PSALM 103:12 NIV

With all my heart I praise the LORD!
I will never forget how kind He has been.
PSALM 103:2 CEV

She was forgiven many, many sins, and so she is very, very grateful.

LUKE 7:47 THE MESSAGE

Jesus, help me to express my love and gratitude to You.
You mean the world to me. Thank You for forgiving me
and setting me free.

NOT SO ORDINARY

The Bible encourages us not to compete for power, position, or influence or to seek the recognition and approval of people the world thinks are "important" (or try to become those people ourselves). The truth is, we are all important to God; each of us is special to Him. Each of us was created by Him to live forever with Him. As C. S. Lewis puts it, "There are no ordinary people. You have never talked to a mere mortal."

Now, not everybody knows it—or acts like it! But what a difference it makes when we do know how special we are to God, when we do act like it—when we live as if it matters, as if we matter. Because we do. And what an impact we can have when we treat others as special, when we show them they matter too.

If you only look at us, you might well miss the brightness. We carry this precious Message around in the unadorned clay pots of our ordinary lives.

II CORINTHIANS 4:7 THE MESSAGE

That's also how it is with people. The ones who stop doing evil and make themselves pure will become special. Their lives will be holy and pleasing to their Master, and they will be able to do all kinds of good deeds.

II TIMOTHY 2:21 CEV

You are the ones chosen by God, chosen for the high calling of priestly work, chosen to be a holy people, God's instruments to do His work and speak out for Him, to tell others of the night-and-day difference He made for you.

I PETER 2:9 THE MESSAGE

*Live in harmony with each other. Don't be too proud to enjoy
the company of ordinary people.*

ROMANS 12:16 NLT

_Lord, let my love for others help them to see
how extraordinary You've created them to be. Help me
to treat them the way You treat me._

PERFECT TIMING

You may not see it—yet. You may not feel it—yet. But God is working right now, today, in your heart and life, in the hearts and lives of those you love, and in the world all around you. One day you will see: He has a plan. Nothing that He allows to happen is random or meaningless or unnecessary. Somehow all of it will serve His greater purpose. And it's a good purpose, a glorious purpose. A purpose that will ultimately bring you great joy as you trust in Him, look to Him, hope in Him. Wait for Him and His purpose to unfold—in His perfect time.

And we know [with great confidence] that God [who is deeply
concerned about us] causes all things to work together [as a plan] for
good for those who love God, to those who are called according to
His plan and purpose.

ROMANS 8:28 AMP

Now, take your stand and see this great thing which the LORD
will do before your eyes.

I SAMUEL 12:16 AMP

He has made everything beautiful in its time.

ECCLESIASTES 3:11 ESV

You are a great and awesome God; You always fulfill Your promises.

DANIEL 9:4 TLB

God, thank You for inviting me—for including me—in Your glorious plans and purposes. Help me to see everything that happens to me with eyes of faith and a heart that trusts.

SAFE AND SOUND

Sometimes we feel as if we're wandering in the dark, lost and alone. Does anyone see? Does anyone know? Does anyone care? God says He sees. He knows. He cares. When we go wandering, He searches for us; He seeks us out. He saves us and surrounds us with His love. He becomes our "hiding place"—our castle or fortress, our stronghold. Our safe space. We don't have to be afraid. Nothing can harm us, because He holds us in His hands. Our hearts and our lives belong to Him—are precious to Him—and He takes the responsibility of caring for us very seriously. Tenderly. Faithfully.

Lord, don't hold back Your tender mercies from me. Let Your unfailing love and faithfulness always protect me.

PSALM 40:11 NLT

You are my hiding place; You will protect me from trouble and surround me with songs of deliverance.

PSALM 32:7 NIV

I know the Lord will continue to rescue me from every trip, trap, snare, and pitfall of evil and carry me safely to His heavenly kingdom. May He be glorified throughout eternity.

II TIMOTHY 4:18 VOICE

The LORD is good, a strength and stronghold in the day of trouble; He knows [He recognizes, cares for, and understands fully] those who take refuge and trust in Him.

NAHUM 1:7 AMP

God, help me to trust in You, to rest in You, to hide in You.

Keep me safe in Your arms today.

MIGHTY WARRIOR

The battle is fierce, but you are not hopeless, helpless, or defenseless. God has equipped you with everything you need to fight and win! He has given you spiritual "armor" to protect you. And faith, hope, courage, strength, grace, truth, love—these are just a few of the powerful weapons with which God has equipped you—not to mention peace, patience, endurance, and so many others. With these weapons, you can overcome fear and doubt; you can defeat discouragement and despair. You can persevere in righteousness (right living) and making wise choices. You can not only survive but thrive in the most difficult challenges of your life. God has made you a mighty warrior, and He is for you!

We are not fighting against flesh-and-blood enemies, but against evil rulers and authorities of the unseen world, against mighty powers in this dark world, and against evil spirits in the heavenly places.

EPHESIANS 6:12 NLT

Therefore, put on the complete armor of God, so that you will be able to [successfully] resist and stand your ground in the evil day [of danger], and having done everything [that the crisis demands], to stand firm [in your place, fully prepared, immovable, victorious].

EPHESIANS 6:13 AMP

Be ready! Let the truth be like a belt around your waist, and let God's justice protect you like armor. Your desire to tell the good news about peace should be like shoes on your feet. Let your faith be like a shield, and you will be able to stop all the flaming arrows of the evil one. Let God's saving power be like a helmet, and for a sword use God's message that comes from the Spirit.

EPHESIANS 6:14—17 CEV

God is strong, and He wants you strong. So take everything the Master has set out for you, well-made weapons of the best materials.

EPHESIANS 6:10–11 THE MESSAGE

God, give me wisdom and courage and strength as I face my battles today. Protect me and defend me and lead me to victory in Jesus's name.

BE GENTLE

Life is hard. You know this. But God is good—and He is gentle with you. Patient, kind, loving, understanding. Be gentle with yourself too. Don't be angry and harsh, impatient or unkind in the way you speak to yourself or treat yourself. Don't punish yourself. Be gentle with yourself.

And while you're being gentle with yourself, be gentle with others. Life is hard for them too. You don't know half of what they're going through. Take every opportunity to be a channel of God's love, mercy, and grace—to pour those good things into the lives of others as God has poured them into you, one blessing after another.

Always be humble and gentle. Be patient with each other, making allowance for each other's faults because of your love.

EPHESIANS 4:2 NLT

The Holy Spirit produces this kind of fruit in our lives: love, joy, peace, patience, kindness, goodness, faithfulness, gentleness, and self-control.

GALATIANS 5:22—23 NLT

Be beautiful inside, in your hearts, with the lasting charm of a gentle and quiet spirit that is so precious to God.

I PETER 3:4 TLB

Blessed [inwardly peaceful, spiritually secure, worthy of respect] are the gentle [the kind-hearted, the sweet-spirited, the self-controlled], for they will inherit the earth.

MATTHEW 5:5 AMP

God, give me Your heart for all those I encounter today. Help me to be loving and patient and kind. Give me the grace to be gentle—for their sake and mine.

GOD'S WORD

God has given us a precious gift—a priceless treasure—in the Bible, the "Word of God." It is His love letter to us, full of encouragement and inspiration, helpful instruction, wisdom, and guidance. Even the challenging parts, the hard stories or the verses that are difficult to understand, in some way they show us who God is or who we are or something else we need to know. And if we ask Him, God will help us to understand. As we read Scripture, He will help us to learn and grow. He will lead us to His truth and teach us to live in the light of His Word.

There's nothing like the written Word of God for showing you the way to salvation through faith in Christ Jesus. Every part of Scripture is God-breathed and useful one way or another—showing us truth, exposing our rebellion, correcting our mistakes, training us to live God's way. Through the Word we are put together and shaped up for the tasks God has for us.

II TIMOTHY 3:16–17 THE MESSAGE

Everything written in the Scriptures was written to teach us, in order that we might have hope through the patience and encouragement which the Scriptures give us.

ROMANS 15:4 GNT

Every word of God can be trusted. He protects those who come to Him for safety.

PROVERBS 30:5 ICB

Your word is a lamp to guide my feet and a light for my path.

PSALM 119:105 NLT

God, thank You for Your Word and the light and life it brings to me. Thank You for teaching me, leading me, and guiding me.

A DOOR OF HOPE

One of the most beautiful, most powerful, most life-giving, life-changing themes in all of Scripture is redemption: God's miraculous ability to transform all our troubles, all our hurts and heartaches, all our grief and pain—even the things that are our own fault, the consequences of our failures and mistakes—into something good. Something meaningful. Something that strengthens, uplifts, and empowers us. Something that blesses, encourages, and inspires others. The Valley of Troubles becomes a Door of Hope, a gateway to something so much greater than we can imagine. So don't give up or give in to despair. Take heart. God is with you. God is for you. Good will come of this someday. Someday soon.

Grace be with you, mercy, and peace.

II JOHN 1:3 KJV

I have heard your prayer and seen your tears; I will heal you.

II KINGS 20:5 NIV

In my desperation I prayed, and the LORD listened;
He saved me from all my troubles.

PSALM 34:6 NLT

There I will give back her vineyards to her and transform her
Valley of Troubles into a Door of Hope.

HOSEA 2:15 TLB

Lord Jesus, give me courage and faith to believe.

My hope and my help come from You.

LOVE THAT LASTS

It's hard to find a love that lasts, a love that will stand the test of time. But that's exactly the kind of love God has for you. His love is steadfast, everlasting; it "endures forever." That means He will never, ever, ever stop loving you. He will never leave you or forsake you. He will never be unfaithful or untrue. He will never betray you.

You mean the world to Him, and He moves heaven and earth to show you. He reveals His love in so many ways, through so many days. He's always whispering to you, reaching for you, and drawing you close. You don't have to keep longing or searching. You can rest in the knowledge that right here, right now, exactly as you are, you are deeply, eternally loved.

O give thanks to the LORD, for He is good,
for His steadfast love endures forever.
PSALM 136:1 NRSV

Many waters cannot quench the flame of love.
SONG OF SOLOMON 8:7 TLB

Love will last forever!
I CORINTHIANS 13:8 NLT

*All the paths of the LORD are lovingkindness and goodness
and truth and faithfulness.*

PSALM 25:10 AMP

---

*Lord, thank You for loving me so deeply, so tenderly,
so faithfully. I can hardly believe it, but I know it's true.
Help me to love You deeply in return.*

FROM THE LIONS' DEN

When Daniel was thrown into the lions' den, he quickly discovered he had company—and not just of the feline variety. God sent a mighty angel to shut the lions' mouths and keep them from making a meal out of Daniel. It's a powerful reminder on our darkest days—when we feel as if we're in the pit, when it seems as if our enemy is about to win—that we are not alone. We are not on our own. God is with us. He is for us. He can do things we can't even imagine; He works in ways we don't understand or think to ask about. His miraculous power will save us. He will rescue us, because we love Him and He loves us.

As for me, I watch in hope for the Lord, I wait for God my Savior;
my God will hear me.

MICAH 7:7 NIV

He is the living God, world without end. His kingdom never falls.
His rule continues eternally. He is a Savior and rescuer. He performs
astonishing miracles in heaven and on earth. He saved Daniel from the
power of the lions.

DANIEL 6:26–27 THE MESSAGE

I know the Lord will continue to rescue me from every trip, trap, snare,
and pitfall of evil and carry me safely to His heavenly kingdom. May He
be glorified throughout eternity.

II TIMOTHY 4:18 VOICE

We do not know what to do, but our eyes are on You.

II CHRONICLES 20:12 NIV

God, You are so good and so great. So mighty to save!
Thank You for coming to my rescue. Thank You for being
with me always.

A REVELATION

Isn't it mind-boggling? The God of the universe has revealed Himself to you—because He wants to be known by you. He wants to be in a relationship with you, one in which you come to know Him the way He already knows you. Fully, completely, deeply, individually, personally, intimately. Let that sink in.

God knows everything about you—every last, little thing—even better than you know yourself. And He wants you to be His friend. The more time you spend with Him, the more you will become like Him, which is wonderful and awesome and amazing, because He Himself is wonderful and awesome and amazing. The more you become like Him, the more your life will encourage others to come to know Him too.

We don't yet see things clearly. We're squinting in a fog, peering through a mist. But it won't be long before the weather clears and the sun shines bright! We'll see it all then, see it all as clearly as God sees us, knowing Him directly just as He knows us!

I CORINTHIANS 13:12 THE MESSAGE

God, who said, "Let light shine out of darkness," made His light shine in our hearts to give us the light of the knowledge of God's glory displayed in the face of Christ.

II CORINTHIANS 4:6 NIV

We can be mirrors that brightly reflect the glory of the Lord. And as the Spirit of the Lord works within us, we become more and more like Him.

II CORINTHIANS 3:18 TLB

Eternal life is to know You, the only true God,
and to know Jesus Christ, the One You sent.

JOHN 17:3 CEV

Lord Jesus, please be with me today. Keep me company on this journey. Hear my heart and help me to find comfort, courage, and strength in You.

LIVE STRONG

It seems like a contradiction, but it's actually true: those moments when we feel the most stressed, the most exhausted, the most empty can be the moments we are the most blessed, the most empowered, and the most full—if we allow the Spirit of God to work in us and through us. When we reach the end of our rope, when we can't hold on a moment longer, we feel as if we've failed. But God rejoices! He's been waiting all this time for us to come to our senses and realize how much we need His help. He's been waiting all this time to help us, if only we will let Him. And when we finally let go, when we start to fall, we find He's right there to catch us, to raise us up in His power and strength to do things we never could have done on our own, let alone imagined!

Trust GOD from the bottom of your heart; don't try to figure out everything on your own. Listen for GOD's voice in everything you do, everywhere you go; He's the one who will keep you on track. Don't assume that you know it all. Run to GOD...

PROVERBS 3:5—7 THE MESSAGE

We stopped relying on ourselves and learned to rely only on God.

II CORINTHIANS 1:9 NLT

What joy for those whose strength comes from the LORD.

PSALM 84:5 NLT

You're blessed when you're at the end of your rope.
With less of you, there is more of God.

MATTHEW 5:3 THE MESSAGE

God, thank You for blessing me with Your love,
Your strength, Your power, Your grace.
Help me to walk in all these things today.

A LOVE STORY

God was heartbroken. His beloved bride (His people) had rejected Him, abandoned Him, and forsaken Him. "She" had turned to other "lovers"—other gods, other things—that seemed more exciting or promised to fulfill all her dreams and desires or meet all her needs. Instead, she found herself betrayed, used and abused by those people and things she thought would help and heal her. She was disappointed and disillusioned.

Although she had turned her back on God, He never turned His back on her, never given up hope that she would come to her senses and come back to Him. He came up with a plan: He would take her back to the place where they first fell in love and remind her of what they once had. He would declare His undying compassion for her again and again until she finally believed it.

One day He would even die for her so she could finally see how much she meant to Him. So His people could see how much they meant to Him. So you could see how much you mean to Him.

He does not punish us for all our sins; He does not deal harshly with us.

PSALM 103:10 NLT

The LORD is merciful! He is kind and patient, and His love never fails.

PSALM 103:8 CEV

So repent [change your inner self—your old way of thinking, regret past sins] and return [to God—seek His purpose for your life], so that your sins may be wiped away [blotted out, completely erased], so that times of refreshing may come from the presence of the Lord [restoring you like a cool wind on a hot day].

ACTS 3:19 AMP

I will win her back once again. I will lead her into the desert
and speak tenderly to her there.

HOSEA 2:14 NLT

Oh, Jesus! Thank You for loving me so faithfully, so tenderly,

so unconditionally. Sometimes my heart wanders and wavers,

but I want to be Yours completely.

BFF

The Bible tells us that Jesus came to be with us—to be one of us—to show us just how much God loved us. He didn't ever want to be separated from us; He didn't want us to be lost and alone. We weren't created to make it on our own. He wanted to be with us, always. He is with us, always—right now, today. He said that when we invite Him, He makes His home in our heart. He comes and lives with us. His Spirit lives in us. We share our heart with Him, and He shares His heart with us. He's the BFF we take with us wherever we go. And He's the best company. We are never without His light, His love, His presence, His peace.

What can we say about all this? If God is on our side, can anyone be against us? God did not keep back His own Son, but He gave Him for us. If God did this, won't He freely give us everything else?

ROMANS 8:31–32 CEV

Now that we are His children,
God has sent the Spirit of His Son into our hearts.

GALATIANS 4:6 CEV

Christ will make His home in your hearts as you trust in Him.
Your roots will grow down into God's love and keep you strong.

EPHESIANS 3:17 NLT

Christ became a human being and lived here on earth among us and was full of loving forgiveness and truth.

JOHN 1:14 TLB

_____
_____
_____
_____
_____
_____
_____
_____
_____
_____
_____
_____
_____
_____

Jesus, please do come and make Your home in me. Live in my heart as I live in Your love. Help me to feel Your presence; fill me with Your peace.

RUNNING TO WIN

Stay focused. There is so much more at stake than a T-shirt or a trophy. What you do—the words you speak, the actions you take, the choices you make—matters. Your life matters. How you run this "race" matters. Every day, you get closer to the finish line, closer to victory, closer to a win that will last for all eternity. But today, there are miles to go. So stay the course and stay alert. Overcome the obstacles and avoid the distractions. Pace yourself. Keep the ultimate goal in mind. Aim for a personal best. Know that God and the angels in heaven and those who have gone before you are all cheering you on!

This is the only race worth running.

II TIMOTHY 4:8 THE MESSAGE

Keep your eyes on Jesus, who both began and finished this race we're in. Study how He did it. Because He never lost sight of where He was headed—that exhilarating finish in and with God—He could put up with anything along the way: Cross, shame, whatever. And now He's there, in the place of honor, right alongside God. When you find yourselves flagging in your faith, go over that story again.

HEBREWS 12:2–3 THE MESSAGE

You know that in a race all the runners run. But only one gets the prize. So run like that. Run to win!

I CORINTHIANS 9:24 ICB

*I'm leaving my old life behind, putting everything on the line for this
mission. I am sprinting toward the only goal that counts: to cross the line,
to win the prize, and to hear God's call to resurrection life found exclusively
in Jesus the Anointed.*

PHILIPPIANS 3:13—14 VOICE

_Lord Jesus, help me to run with perseverance, courage,
and determination. Give me the strength to accomplish the mission—
all that You have planned and purposed for me._

SUCH A COMFORT

Redemption is God's specialty. He is able to transform all our loss, grief, and pain into something beautiful, powerful, and profound. In our suffering, He holds us close, so close. And then He takes what feels random and meaningless and cruel and turns it into significant, purposeful passion—or compassion. Comfort. Care. In time, the grief we've gone through gives us not only the tenderness but the wisdom, experience, and authority to speak into the lives of others. It rouses us to action and motivates us to create change and make meaningful differences in many other hearts and lives. What a comfort to know that, even now, God is working all these things for our good.

You will not be overwhelmed with grief like those who live
outside of the true hope.
I THESSALONIANS 4:13 VOICE

Blessed [gratefully praised and adored] be the God and Father of our
Lord Jesus Christ, the Father of mercies and the God of all comfort.
II CORINTHIANS 1:3 AMP

He comes alongside us when we go through hard times, and before you
know it, He brings us alongside someone else who is going through hard
times so that we can be there for that person just as God was there for us.
II CORINTHIANS 1:4 THE MESSAGE

Rejoice with those who rejoice; mourn with those who mourn.

ROMANS 12:15 NIV

Lord, please heal my hurting heart; redeem my pain and suffering. Open my eyes to the hurting hearts around me and help me to be a healing presence.

THAT'S EVERYTHING

God hasn't forgotten anything. He hasn't left anything out. He has provided generously, abundantly, above and beyond what you could ask or even imagine. You have everything you need to live how He's called you to live, to do what He's called you to do—everything you need to love and lead and give and serve the people He's called you to. Whatever you feel you're short on, whenever you feel you're running out or running low, just ask Him. Ask Him to show you what He already has stored up for you, what He's ready and willing to give you, to equip you. You will find it more than enough.

If you trust the LORD, you will never miss out on anything good.

PSALM 34:10 CEV

Your Father knows the things you need before you ask Him.

MATTHEW 6:8 ICB

Have faith in God, who is rich and blesses us with everything
we need to enjoy life.

I TIMOTHY 6:17 CEV

By His divine power, God has given us everything we need for living a godly life.

II PETER 1:3 NLT

Lord Jesus, thank You for providing everything I need.

Thank You for equipping me and empowering me.

Help me to honor You in everything I say and do.

HEART HUNGER

It's a good thing to be hungry—hungry for God, that is. It's good to want to know Him more and more, to want to experience His love, His power, His peace, His presence. It's a good thing to be hungry for truth and goodness and justice, to desire to do what's right ourselves and to see others do what's right as well. This kind of heart hunger motivates us to take action and make changes—and make a difference. It inspires us to be part of the solution rather than the problem. It gives us perspective and helps us keep our priorities straight. But more than anything, allowing ourselves to be hungry—to feel the emptiness within—prepares us to receive the blessings that come when we are filled. God promises to meet our every need, to "feed" us and fill us with good things. Ultimately, we find our deepest satisfaction, our greatest fulfillment, in Him.

O God, You are my God; I earnestly search for You. My soul thirsts for You; my whole body longs for You in this parched and weary land where there is no water.

PSALM 63:1 NLT

You open Your hand and satisfy the desires of every living thing.

PSALM 145:16 NIV

That's why I will speak of Your righteousness and sing praises to You all day long.

PSALM 35:28 VOICE

Blessed are those who hunger and thirst for righteousness, for they will be filled.

MATTHEW 5:6 NIV

Lord, help me not to stuff myself with empty things but to feel

the deep hunger that can only be satisfied by You.

LOOK AND LEAP

You were made to be beautiful and strong, confident and courageous, graceful and swift and agile—like a deer dancing across the mountain heights. God Himself has created you to be everything you need to be to live the life He's called you to and to fulfill His plans and purposes for you.

Don't worry obsessively over the challenges and obstacles ahead of you. Don't live in regret over past stumbles or tremble in fear while looking down at the next steps. Don't look down at all. Look up! Lift your eyes and look to Him. Trust Him. Draw your strength from His strength—and leap!

I cried out, "I am slipping!" but your unfailing love,
O LORD, supported me.
PSALM 94:18 NLT

He made me sure-footed as a deer and placed me high up
where I am safe.
PSALM 18:33 VOICE

How beautiful on the mountains are the feet of the messenger who
brings good news, the good news of peace and salvation, the news that
the God of Israel reigns!
ISAIAH 52:7 NLT

The Lord GOD is my strength [my source of courage, my invincible army]; He has made my feet [steady and sure] like hinds' feet and makes me walk [forward with spiritual confidence] on my high places [of challenge and responsibility].

HABAKKUK 3:19 AMP

Lord God, thank You for the strength and grace You have given me and the courage and confidence to fulfill my calling. Lead me to new heights today!

WILLING AND WAITING

Waiting is one of the hardest things God asks us to do. We're people of action, not all that patient by nature. How often have we thought to ourselves—or said to someone else—"Don't just stand there! Do something!" But sometimes all we can do is stand there. Stand in hope, stand in faith. Stand in the knowledge that God is at work. He keeps His promises. Answers are on the way. And His timing is perfect. When you think about it, "waiting" can be an active choice: we're choosing to stay focused, intentional, and purposeful. We're keeping our eyes open to see what God is doing; our ears are open to hear what He might say. We're standing ready to answer His call, ready to obey.

Don't give up. Wait for the Eternal in expectation, and be strong. Again, wait for the Eternal.

PSALM 27:14 VOICE

Do you not know? Have you not heard? The LORD is the everlasting God, the Creator of the ends of the earth.

ISAIAH 40:28 NIV

Those who wait for the LORD [who expect, look for, and hope in Him] will gain new strength and renew their power; they will lift up their wings [and rise up close to God] like eagles [rising toward the sun]; they will run and not become weary, they will walk and not grow tired.

ISAIAH 40:31 AMP

We wait [expectantly] for the LORD; He is our help.

PSALM 33:20 AMP

God, I know I can trust You to work in my heart and life today—and in the hearts and lives of those I love. Whatever it takes, I'm waiting in hope, in confidence, in faith.

THIS LOVE

How God longs for you! How He loves you! You are so beautiful, so special, so precious to Him. He wants to spend time with you—to talk and to listen. He is constantly calling you into relationship with Him, inviting you into intimacy with Him. He knows about all the things that compete for your love and devotion, your time and attention. He understands the distractions and interruptions. But love won't let Him walk away and leave you with lesser things.

He keeps coming to you, keeps calling to you, keeps finding ways to attract your attention. He knows that nothing will be as meaningful, as significant, as fulfilling as the time you share or the connection you create. Nothing will comfort or strengthen or energize you more. Nothing will bring you greater joy. It's for this love that He created you.

My heart has heard You say, "Come and talk with Me." And my heart responds, "LORD, I am coming."

PSALM 27:8 NLT

My soul yearns, even faints, for the courts of the LORD; my heart and my flesh cry out for the Living God.

PSALM 84:2 NIV

Being with You will fill me with joy.

PSALM 16:11 ICB

Let me see your face, let me hear your voice; for your voice is sweet,
and your face is lovely.

SONG OF SOLOMON 2:14 AMP

Lord, You are the love of my life. Thank You for each moment together, each day, each year. Let me grow deeper and deeper in love with You.

A FAITHFUL FRIEND

Friendship is one of the greatest gifts God has given us. It means that none of us has to go through life alone. We have Him and we have each other! Not that friendship is always easy. In some ways, we are all broken and hurting people, and sometimes, in our brokenness, we hurt other people. We disappoint them or let them down, the same way they do us. It can take a lot of love, a lot of forgiveness, a lot of grace—and the willingness to put real work into our relationships. But it's so worth it. What if you're in a season where you can't find a faithful friend? Ask God to show you someone who needs one.

This is My command: Love one another the way I loved you. This is the very best way to love. Put your life on the line for your friends. You are My friends when you do the things I command you.

JOHN 15:12—14 THE MESSAGE

Beloved, let us [unselfishly] love and seek the best for one another, for love is from God; and everyone who loves [others] is born of God and knows God [through personal experience].

I JOHN 4:7 AMP

A friend loves at all times.

PROVERBS 17:17 NIV

All people will know that you are My followers if you love each other.

JOHN 13:35 NCV

God, thank You for being my friend.

Thank You for the friends You've given me.

Help me to be a loving and faithful friend to others.

SEEN AND HEARD

Imagine being introduced to Jesus—meeting Him in person for the first time—and hearing Him say that He already knew you. Discovering that He really did know all about you, all the secrets of your heart, that He even heard your personal, private thoughts and prayers earlier that morning... That's what happened to Nathanael in the Bible. It was mind-blowing for him, just as it's mind-blowing for us today to be seen and known this way.

It's not always a comfortable feeling, being so transparent, so vulnerable and exposed. And yet, if we let it, it can be incredibly reassuring. Because Jesus says He not only sees us and knows us, He loves us—unconditionally. We don't have to carefully manage our brand or project the perfect image. We can be real with Him. He is real with us.

He knows about everyone, everywhere. Everything about us is bare and wide open to the all-seeing eyes of our living God.

HEBREWS 4:13 TLB

Yes, He knows the secrets of every heart.

PSALM 44:21 TLB

We do not have a High Priest who is unable to sympathize and understand our weaknesses and temptations, but One who has been tempted [knowing exactly how it feels to be human] in every respect as we are, yet without [committing any] sin. Therefore let us [with privilege] approach the throne of grace [that is, the throne of God's gracious favor] with confidence and without fear, so that we may receive mercy [for our failures] and find [His amazing] grace to help in time of need [an appropriate blessing, coming just at the right moment].

HEBREWS 4:15—16 AMP

"How do you know me?" Nathanael asked. Jesus answered,
"I saw you while you were still under the fig tree."

JOHN 1:48 NIV

_____
_____
_____
_____
_____
_____
_____
_____
_____
_____
_____
_____
_____
_____

Jesus, thank You for seeing me, knowing me, loving me.
Help me to see You, know You, and love You faithfully.

GREATER THINGS

Jesus says that when we give our heart and life to Him, He will use us to do great things—greater, even, than the things He did when He was here on earth. Can you imagine? Think about the kinds of things Jesus did: He saw people for who they really were, loved them, listened to them, forgave them, and helped them. He healed them. He challenged them. He comforted them. He met their physical, emotional, and spiritual needs. He showed them who God is and how much God loves them.

How can we, as human beings, possibly do all these things—and even "greater"? By the power of God's Holy Spirit, working in and through us, giving us the compassion, the wisdom, the patience, the sensitivity (not to mention the energy!), to be available to the people He sends us to. The people He has called us to reach. It's such an important task, but we can do it in His strength, by His grace, for His glory.

It is God Himself who has made us what we are and given us new lives from Christ Jesus; and long ages ago He planned that we should spend these lives in helping others.

EPHESIANS 2:10 TLB

God is always fair. He will remember how you helped His people in the past and how you are still helping them. You belong to God, and He won't forget the love you have shown His people.

HEBREWS 6:10 CEV

The one who blesses others is abundantly blessed; those who help others are helped.

PROVERBS 11:25 THE MESSAGE

I am telling you the truth: those who believe in Me will do what I do—
yes, they will do even greater things.

JOHN 14:12 GNT

Lord, show me the people You have called me to help.

Pour Your healing power into their hearts and lives through me.

A NEW DAY

As the irrepressible heroine of Anne of Green Gables exclaims, "Isn't it nice to think that tomorrow is a new day with no mistakes in it yet?" Yes! But we don't have to wait for tomorrow—or Monday or the beginning of a new month or year—to start fresh. It doesn't matter how many times we've stumbled, how many times we've fallen or failed in the past. It doesn't matter how many mistakes we made yesterday or even five minutes ago. Morning by morning, moment by moment, God's mercies are new. His forgiveness is real. His grace is sufficient. With courage and confidence, we can begin again. Right now. In this moment. It's a new day.

As high as heaven is over the earth, so strong is His love to those who
fear Him. And as far as sunrise is from sunset, He has separated us
from our sins.
PSALM 103:11—12 THE MESSAGE

Now we rejoice in our wonderful new relationship with God—
all because of what our Lord Jesus Christ has done in dying for our
sins—making us friends of God.
ROMANS 5:11 TLB

The humble will be filled with fresh joy from the LORD.
ISAIAH 29:19 NLT

Great is His faithfulness; His mercies begin afresh each morning.

LAMENTATIONS 3:23 NLT

Lord Jesus, thank You for forgiving all my sin—every bit of it. Help me to let go of the past, start fresh, and live joyfully today in the light of Your love, Your mercy, and Your grace.

UNFORGETTABLE

Sometimes other people forget you—forget your name, forget you met. Forget to call or text. Forget to like or comment. Accidentally leave you off the invite list. It's true. Even people you love—who are supposed to love you—may not always think of you and may not always remember you.

But God will. God will remember you. He says that nothing on earth could make Him forget how much He loves you. Nothing could make Him forget how special you are to Him. He knows you inside and out. After all, He created you. You are His precious child. He is always thinking of you. To Him, you are unforgettable.

Can a woman forget her own baby and not love the child she bore?
Even if a mother should forget her child, I will never forget you.
ISAIAH 49:15 GNT

I, the LORD, made you, and I will not forget you.
ISAIAH 44:21 NLT

The LORD remembers us and will bless us.
PSALM 115:12 NLT

Jesus, remember me when You come into Your Kingdom.

LUKE 23:42 NLT

_____

_____

_____

_____

_____

_____

_____

_____

_____

_____

_____

_____

_____

_____

God, thank You for always thinking of me,

always remembering me, always caring for me.

Your faithful love is such a comfort to me.

THE CALL OF ADVENTURE

God created you with a specific plan and purpose in mind. A mission. A calling. There are things He specifically designed for you—and specifically designed for you to do, things that will bring you deep joy, profound meaning, and fulfillment. If you say yes. If you are willing. Will you believe? Will you trust? Will you receive and respond to His invitation?

It's the adventure of a lifetime. There will be battles to fight (and win), challenges and obstacles to overcome. But you won't have to go it alone. Not one single step. He will be with you all the way. He will work in you and through you. He will guide you and comfort you. He will provide everything you need. God Himself will enable you and empower you to accomplish this mission for His kingdom and glory.

Then I heard the voice of the Lord saying, "Whom shall I send? And who will go for us?" And I said, "Here am I. Send me!"

ISAIAH 6:8 NIV

Just think—you don't need a thing, you've got it all! All God's gifts are right in front of you as you wait expectantly for our Master Jesus to arrive on the scene for the Finale. And not only that, but God Himself is right alongside to keep you steady and on track until things are all wrapped up by Jesus. God, who got you started in this spiritual adventure, shares with us the life of His Son and our Master Jesus. He will never give up on you. Never forget that.

I CORINTHIANS 1:7—9 THE MESSAGE

You will do everything You have promised; LORD, Your love is eternal.
Complete the work that You have begun.

PSALM 138:8 GNT

Jesus, help me to embrace the adventure, to step out in faith and answer Your call. Fulfill all Your plans and purposes for me. I believe.

HE WILL CARRY YOU

They may seem like tiny bundles of endless energy, but even the most enthusiastic toddlers grow tired eventually. They get overwhelmed by crowds or noise, frightened by things that seem unfamiliar or threatening. On long journeys, their little legs give out. They need someone stronger to scoop them up and carry them. To give them rest. To hold them close and remind them that they're safe and loved.

That's just what your heavenly Father does with you. Life's journey can be long and hard. Sometimes you get hot and tired and cranky, frightened or overwhelmed or stressed, or in desperate need of rest. That's when He scoops you up in His big, strong arms and invites you to tell Him all about it. He listens carefully. He holds you close and whispers—or sings—softly, to soothe your troubled heart. He reminds you that you are safe. He will carry you. You can rest in His love.

I, your GOD, have a firm grip on you and I'm not letting go.
I'm telling you, "Don't panic. I'm right here to help you."
ISAIAH 41:13 THE MESSAGE

Show love to the LORD your God by walking in His ways
and holding tightly to Him.
DEUTERONOMY 11:22 NLT

Casting all your cares [all your anxieties, all your worries, and all your
concerns, once and for all] on Him, for He cares about you [with deepest
affection, and watches over you very carefully].
I PETER 5:7 AMP

*There you saw how the L*ORD *your God carried you, as a father carries his son.*

DEUTERONOMY 1:31 NIV

Father God, remind me to come to You—to run to You—

and find rest in You today.

CHOICES, CHOICES

Decision fatigue—it's a very real thing. We have so many choices to make on a daily basis, so many options. We have so much more information at our fingertips and so much more flexibility than any previous generation. But somehow it can all be paralyzing. What do we do with this much information—and all this freedom? How do we choose the best option or make the wisest decision? How do we know which way to go when there are so many ways—and so many opinions? Thankfully, we're not alone—or on our own. God's people have always prayed for wisdom and direction, asking Him to show them the way as they navigated all kinds of decisions, difficult questions, and challenging circumstances. And God answered them. He has helped them. He will answer you and help you too.

God, teach me lessons for living so I can stay the course. Give me insight so I can do what You tell me—my whole life one long, obedient response.
PSALM 119:33 THE MESSAGE

I will give you what you asked for! I will give you a wise and understanding heart.
I KINGS 3:12 NLT

I am guiding you in wisdom. And I am leading you to do what is right.
PROVERBS 4:11 ICB

The Lord says, "I will make you wise. I will show you where to go.
I will guide you and watch over you."

PSALM 32:8 ICB

Lord, show me the way. Guide me in my choices today.

Help me to see where You want me to be—and give me courage to

follow wherever You lead.

HAVE MERCY

Let's face it: we've all messed up, made mistakes, or been thoughtless or careless or clueless. Sometimes we've even been deliberately reckless, rebellious, stubborn, or foolish. And God—in His great love for us—has shown us mercy. He has responded to us not with anger or frustration or irritation, but with compassion, gentleness, and patience. No, He has not treated us as our sins deserve; instead, He has completely forgiven us. Though we were the ones in the wrong, He has taken the initiative to reach out and make things right between us. We have been blessed, and we'll continue to be blessed as we show this same mercy to others. The more mercy we have, the more we'll be given. The more we'll be forgiven. The more we'll experience His unending mercy and amazing grace.

Whenever you stand praying, if you have anything against anyone, forgive him [drop the issue, let it go], so that your Father who is in heaven will also forgive you your transgressions and wrongdoings [against Him and others].

MARK 11:25 AMP

Yes, you must show mercy to others, or God will not show mercy to you.

JAMES 2:13 ICB

Since God chose you to be the holy people He loves, you must clothe yourselves with tenderhearted mercy, kindness, humility, gentleness, and patience.

COLOSSIANS 3:12 NLT

Blessed are the merciful, for they will be shown mercy.

MATTHEW 5:7 NIV

God, thank You for all the grace and mercy You've shown me. Help me to show that same mercy to others. Let me pass on this gift and blessing.

JUST ASK

It's okay that you don't have all the answers. It's true that no matter how smart you are (or how smart your phone is), you can't figure it all out on your own. But you don't have to. You have something so much more powerful than a search engine or a survey or crowdsourcing. You have all-access to the ultimate content Creator, the Source of all knowledge, wisdom, and truth. You have His Spirit to lead you and guide you. Your Father really does know best. All you have to do is ask.

When you come to Him, He will never say, "How many times do I have to tell you?" He will never complain, "Why can't you figure this out for yourself?" He has all the answers, and He wants you to ask. He waits for you to ask. He loves you—and He loves helping you!

If you want to know what God wants you to do, ask Him, and He will gladly tell you, for He is always ready to give a bountiful supply of wisdom to all who ask Him.

JAMES 1:5 TLB

His name we'll know in many ways—He will be called Wonderful Counselor, Mighty God, Dear Father everlasting, ever-present never-failing, Master of Wholeness, Prince of Peace.

ISAIAH 9:6 VOICE

When the Friend comes, the Spirit of the Truth, He will take you by the hand and guide you into all the truth there is. He won't draw attention to Himself, but will make sense out of what is about to happen and, indeed, out of all that I have done and said.

JOHN 16:13 THE MESSAGE

God alone understands the way to wisdom;
He knows where it can be found.

JOB 28:23 NLT

Father, thank You for always being there for me—always ready and willing to help me. Show me what I need to know today and help me find my way.

NOT WITHOUT HOPE

Things looked pretty hopeless from where Jonah sat—in the belly of a "great fish." The prophet had resisted God's voice, rebelled against God's plan, and run (as if it were possible to run) as far away from God as he knew how ... only to end up storm-tossed, shipwrecked, and swallowed up by the sea. But things weren't as hopeless as they seemed. In his darkest moment, Jonah knew one thing to do: run to God instead of from Him. Ask God for help. Admit to making mistakes. Ask Him for mercy, forgiveness, and grace. Receive His salvation and live to serve another day.

From a sea of troubles, I call out to You, Lord.
Won't You please listen as I beg for mercy?

PSALM 130:1—2 CEV

Lord, if You kept a record of our sins, who, O Lord, could ever survive?

PSALM 130:3 NLT

Those who cling to worthless idols turn away from God's love for them.
But I, with shouts of grateful praise, will sacrifice to You. What I have
vowed I will make good. I will say, "Salvation comes from the Lord."

JONAH 2:8—9 NIV

Bring us back to You, God. Turn the light of Your face upon us so that we will be rescued from this sea of darkness.

PSALM 80:3 VOICE

Lord, You are my only hope! My Savior!

I'm calling on You today. Meet me where I am

and help me get to where You want me to be.

BELOVED

It's easy to forget who we are sometimes. We put our identities in our careers or in our family roles, but the truth is, we are so much more than the titles we are given. God says He calls us by name. We are His children. And He loves us unconditionally.

That is our reality. That is *the* reality. We are God's precious children—created by Him, loved by Him, chosen by Him. The world tries to make us see things differently—tries to convince us that we aren't worth anything unless we have (or do) *x*, *y*, and *z*. But God says we don't have to do anything. We just have to *be*. We don't have to have anything. We *already* have everything. We have Him. We don't need to fit in. We belong. And we are beloved.

The Spirit you have received adopts you and welcomes you into God's own family. That's why we call out to Him, "Abba! Father!" as we would address a loving daddy.

ROMANS 8:15 VOICE

My dear children, you come from God and belong to God. You have already won a big victory ... for the Spirit in you is far stronger than anything in the world.

I JOHN 4:4 THE MESSAGE

Watch what God does, and then you do it, like children who learn proper behavior from their parents. Mostly what God does is love you. Keep company with Him and learn a life of love. Observe how Christ loved us. His love was not cautious but extravagant. He didn't love in order to get something from us but to give everything of Himself to us. Love like that.

EPHESIANS 5:1—2 THE MESSAGE

See how much the Father has loved us! His love is so great that we are called God's children—and so, in fact, we are.

I JOHN 3:1 GNT

_____

_____

_____

_____

_____

_____

_____

_____

_____

_____

_____

God, thank You for constantly reminding me how much You love me. Thank You for showing me what that love looks like—and helping me love others the same way.

STANDING IN THE GAP

God's people returned to their homeland after years in exile only to find their cities in ruins and the walls in desperate need of repair. As they set to work rebuilding, they faced constant threats, harassment, and intimidation from enemies who did not want to see the nation grow strong and healthy and prosperous once again. The people were often tempted to give in to fear and discouragement. But their leader, Nehemiah, reminded them that they were not alone. God was with them, and they had each other. Nehemiah placed teams in each of the gaps in the walls. They took turns: some team members focused on making repairs while the others stood guard, with weapons drawn, ready to defend against any attack of the enemy.

God calls us to do the same today: work together and take turns standing in the gap for each other, supporting and strengthening one another through hard times. Together we will overcome the enemy and experience victory!

Stand united, singular in vision, contending for people's trust in the Message, the good news, not flinching or dodging in the slightest before the opposition. Your courage and unity will show them what they're up against: defeat for them, victory for you—and both because of God.

PHILIPPIANS 1:28–29 THE MESSAGE

Help each other with your troubles.

GALATIANS 6:2 ICB

Don't be afraid of the enemy! Remember the Lord, who is great and glorious, and fight.

NEHEMIAH 4:14 NLT

*Take up your positions; stand firm and
see the deliverance the L ORD will give you.*

II CHRONICLES 20:17 NIV

---

*Jesus, show me where I can stand with someone else today—
how I can support and strengthen them, as others do the same
for me. Give us courage and bring us victory.*

THE REAL YOU

Jesus is never disappointed in you. Read that sentence again: Jesus is never disappointed in you. Think about it: to be disappointed, He'd have to have expected better. But unlike you, He doesn't have unrealistic expectations of you. He doesn't hold you to the same impossible standards you set for yourself. He isn't desperately hoping that somehow you'll do better or be better than you really are.

He knows exactly who you are. He knows exactly how "weak" and imperfect you are. But He's the One who chose to make you human and vulnerable and real—and He embraces all that comes with it. He is gentle and tender with you. Patient and forgiving. He has such compassion for you and all you're going through. Better than anybody else, He knows how hard it is for you to be you. So take a deep breath, shake off the weight of guilt and shame, and rest in His deep love for you today.

He will not crush the weakest reed or put out a flickering candle.

MATTHEW 12:20 NLT

He knows how we were made. He remembers that we are dust.

PSALM 103:14 ICB

Our bodies are buried in brokenness, but they will be raised in glory.
They are buried in weakness, but they will be raised in strength.

I CORINTHIANS 15:43 NLT

Jesus understands every weakness of ours,
because He was tempted in every way that we are.

HEBREWS 4:15 CEV

Jesus, thank You for loving me—the real me—so fully and
completely. Thank You for being so kind and patient with me.
Help me, in my weakness, to bring You glory.

A VIP

Who you are is so much more than what you look like or the image you project. Your value, your significance, your importance and impact are so much more than you can measure in likes or follows or number of friends. You are already a VIP! You make an extraordinary difference in the world just by being who God created you to be, embracing what makes you uniquely you, and leaning into your calling. Whether you realize it, your influence is deeply felt in your home, your school or workplace, your church, and your community. Online and in real life, you set an example. Everyone you interact with on a daily basis can be blessed, encouraged, challenged, comforted, or inspired … touched by the God who lives and works in and through you.

Be all the more diligent to make certain about His calling and choosing
you [be sure that your behavior reflects and confirms your relationship
with God]; for by doing these things [actively developing these virtues],
you will never stumble [in your spiritual growth and will live a life that
leads others away from sin].

II PETER 1:10 AMP

What matters is not your outer appearance—the styling of your hair, the
jewelry you wear, the cut of your clothes—but your inner disposition.
Cultivate inner beauty, the gentle, gracious kind that God delights in.
The holy women of old were beautiful before God that way.

I PETER 3:3–5 THE MESSAGE

Charm is deceptive, and beauty is fleeting;
but a woman who fears the LORD is to be praised.

PROVERBS 31:30 NIV

An excellent woman [one who is spiritual, capable, intelligent,
and virtuous]...her value is more precious than jewels and her worth
is far above rubies or pearls.

PROVERBS 31:10 AMP

Thank You for the ways You are already using me.
Help me to stay focused on what really matters in this life
and to make the most of every opportunity You give me.

GOD MEANT IT FOR GOOD

The Bible tells us that Joseph's own brothers ambushed him, beat him, and sold him into slavery in Egypt. But he could let go of the hurt and bitterness he felt over his brothers' betrayal because he saw God's hand in everything that happened to him. Suddenly a series of miraculous events put him in a position second only to Pharaoh. He was given both the wisdom and the power to save millions of people from famine and death, including his own family. And he knew it had been a part of God's plan all along. One day, like Joseph, we too will see that though others have intended to harm us and Satan has tried to destroy us, God has been working everything together for our good.

Be gentle and ready to forgive; never hold grudges. Remember, the Lord forgave you, so you must forgive others.

COLOSSIANS 3:13 TLB

You meant evil against me, but God meant it for good.

GENESIS 50:20 ESV

We are confident that God is able to orchestrate everything to work toward something good and beautiful when we love Him and accept His invitation to live according to His plan.

ROMANS 8:28 VOICE

*"My thoughts are nothing like your thoughts," says the Lord.
"And my ways are far beyond anything you could imagine."*

ISAIAH 55:8 NLT

*Jesus, help me to forgive others as You have forgiven me,
trusting that You can turn every grief and pain, every loss,
every wound, into something good and beautiful for Your glory.*

SPECIAL AGENT

When was the last time you felt special? Was it a few hours ago, a few days, or longer? What made you feel that way? Was it something someone said? Something you read? A gift or compliment or some encouragement you received? You know how much it means to you when you're reminded of a truth that's not always easy to believe: you are special, just the way God made you, just by being you. You have a special place in His heart. And you matter. You make a difference.

Take a few moments to think about how you can pass on the blessing—how you can be an "agent" of God's love, mercy, and grace and share this truth today. Pray about it and ask God to show you what you can do to remind someone else that they're special.

You are very precious to God. Peace! Be encouraged! Be strong!
DANIEL 10:19 NLT

You, beloved, are the light of the world.
MATTHEW 5:14 VOICE

Love each other deeply with all your heart.
I PETER 1:22 NCV

You have a special place in my heart.

PHILIPPIANS 1:7 CEV

Lord, help me to shine with the light of Your love,

and let that light, that love be an encouragement to someone else.

Let them know how special they are to You.

JESUS CALLING

God met Moses in the desert, calling to him out of a burning bush—which certainly got his attention! The reason: God had a plan and a purpose for Moses. His people were suffering in slavery in Egypt. God wanted to send Moses to set His people free.

God wants to use us to set people free today too, sharing with them the freedom we've found through our faith in Jesus. He calls us to rescue those who are lost or in danger, to take action on behalf of the helpless, the poor, and the weak. If we are willing to say yes, He will show us where He wants to send us. He will open our eyes to people in need. And He will give us all the strength, wisdom, grace, and courage we need.

Those of us who are strong and able in the faith need to step in and lend a hand to those who falter, and not just do what is most convenient for us. Strength is for service, not status. Each one of us needs to look after the good of the people around us, asking ourselves, "How can I help?"
ROMANS 15:1–2 THE MESSAGE

Try to help those who argue against you. Be merciful to those who doubt. Save some by snatching them as from the very flames of hell itself. And as for others, help them to find the Lord by being kind to them.
JUDE 1:22–23 TLB

Rescue the perishing; don't hesitate to step in and help.
PROVERBS 24:11 THE MESSAGE

The LORD said, "I have indeed seen the misery of my people.... I have heard them crying out ... and I am concerned about their suffering."

EXODUS 3:7 NIV

Lord, show me how to answer Your call. Fulfill Your plans and purposes for me. Show me the people You want me to love and serve and set free.

BE STILL

On our hard days and in our heartaches, in our loneliness, worry, and fear, God longs to comfort us. He wants to hold us close, to "gather us under His wings," wrap us up in His arms, cradle us in His lap. Like the most kind and compassionate father, the most tender and loving mother, He feels deeply for His children. He hurts when we hurt. And He wants to help. Too often we're too busy kicking and screaming, wriggling and writhing and pulling away, like a toddler in a tantrum. We don't even see the arms that wait to welcome us; we don't hear the love that speaks so softly and seeks to soothe our troubled hearts. But if we can learn—when we feel ourselves swirling in a whirlwind of emotion—to stop, take a breath, and look up, we will find peace. We will find comfort. We will find rest. God is ready and willing to give us all we need.

Be still, and know that I am God!
PSALM 46:10 NLT

I will comfort you as a mother comforts her child.
ISAIAH 66:13 NCV

I have learned to feel safe and satisfied, just like a young child on its mother's lap.
PSALM 131:2 CEV

O Jerusalem, Jerusalem...! How often I have wanted to gather
your children together as a hen protects her chicks beneath her wings,
but you wouldn't let Me.

MATTHEW 23:37 NLT

God, You are so good to me. How You comfort me!

When my heart hurts, when I'm worried or afraid,

help me to be still and know Your love and Your peace.

BATTLE-READY

Life is full of challenges—"battles"—we must face. (Sometimes it even feels like all-out war!) But we don't come to the battlefield unprepared or unequipped. God says He uses everything that happens to us to teach us, train us, strengthen us, and prepare us for whatever's coming next.

In a very real sense, we're always either in boot camp or in battle. But He promises that we will never find ourselves defenseless against the enemy. He'll supply the strategy, the skill, and the power, as well as the courage and the strength. And He Himself is our Captain and Commander. He will fight for us, fight beside us, and lead us to victory.

My power and my strength come from the LORD, and He has saved me.
PSALM 118:14 CEV

I can do all things [which He has called me to do] through Him who strengthens and empowers me [to fulfill His purpose—I am self-sufficient in Christ's sufficiency; I am ready for anything and equal to anything through Him who infuses me with inner strength and confident peace.]
PHILIPPIANS 4:13 AMP

You have given me Your shield of victory. Your right hand supports me; Your help has made me great.
PSALM 18:35 NLT

He trains my hands for battle; my arms can bend a bow of bronze.

PSALM 18:34 NIV

---

*Thank You, Jesus, for the strength You've given me—
and for the victory! All the glory and honor belong to You!*

PURE IN HEART

What does it mean to be "pure in heart"? Something that is pure is clean and clear, unpolluted and uncontaminated. Genuine and authentic. Innocent. Sometimes our hearts don't feel very pure. We have all kinds of conflicting thoughts and feelings, hidden agendas, and ulterior motives. Layer upon layer upon layer.

But Jesus tells us that with His death on the cross, He has cut through all those layers. He has cleansed us of all our impurities. In the deepest part of us, in the very heart of us, He has made us clean and new. And because of this, we can see God. We can know God. We can be in relationship with Him. We can experience His presence, His peace, and His power at work in us and through us. We can also learn to make choices that protect our heart and protect the work that God has done. We're no longer stuck in the muck and mire of our old ways. We are blessed to have the freedom to walk in obedience to His Word.

Truly God is good to His people ... to those with pure hearts.

PSALM 73:1 VOICE

He offered Himself as a sacrifice to free us from a dark, rebellious life into this good, pure life, making us a people He can be proud of, energetic in goodness.

TITUS 2:14 THE MESSAGE

So, beloved, since you are looking forward to these things, be diligent and make every effort to be found by Him [at His return] spotless and blameless, in peace [that is, inwardly calm with a sense of spiritual well-being and confidence, having lived a life of obedience to Him].

II PETER 3:14 AMP

Blessed are the pure in heart, for they will see God.

MATTHEW 5:8 NIV

Lord Jesus, thank You for the blessing of a pure heart. Everywhere I go, in everything I do, help me to see You.

LEARNING TO LISTEN

Sometimes we ask God for a sign. We ask Him to speak into our lives, to show us where to go or what to do or how to decide. We want His help—we need His help—and He's promised to provide it. He's promised to lead us and guide us. But we're afraid we'll miss it! We want something big and flashy and dramatic, something that shouts: "This way!" or "Yes!" or "No!"

Sometimes we get it. Sometimes God shouts. But often He whispers. He speaks to us in the stillness and the quiet, in the ordinary and the everyday. He gently nudges us in the right direction. He understands how important it is to us. It's important to Him too. He knows how easily we get confused or distracted, and one way or another, He will make it clear. He's teaching us to hear His voice. He knows we're still learning to listen.

Your ears will hear sweet words behind you: "Go this way. There is your path; this is how you should go" whenever you must decide whether to turn to the right or the left.

ISAIAH 30:21 VOICE

Love the LORD your God, listen to His voice, and hold fast to Him.

DEUTERONOMY 30:20 NIV

This God is our God for ever and ever;
He will be our guide even to the end.

PSALM 48:14 NIV

Then a very strong wind blew.... But the Lord was not in the wind. After the wind, there was an earthquake. But the Lord was not in the earthquake. After the earthquake, there was a fire. But the Lord was not in the fire. After the fire, there was a quiet, gentle voice.

1 KINGS 19:11—12 ICB

Speak, Lord; I'm listening. Open my heart and mind, my eyes and ears. Help me to hear Your voice and trust what You're saying.

CHOOSE HOPE

Sometimes you have to take a stand. You have to choose whether you're going to live in faith or doubt, courage or fear, hope or despair. You have to choose to believe that God is who He says He is, that He loves you like He says He does, that He keeps every one of His promises. Even when you can't see it, even when you can't feel it, even when others give in and give up and walk away, you're here to stay. You're here to praise, to rejoice, to give thanks for all the blessings and miracles and answers to prayer you've already been given—and for those you know are on the way.

Even though the fig trees have no blossoms, and there are no grapes on the vines; even though the olive crop fails, and the fields lie empty and barren; even though the flocks die in the fields, and the cattle barns are empty, yet I will rejoice in the LORD! I will be joyful in the God of my salvation!

HABAKKUK 3:17–18 NLT

I remain confident of this: I will see the goodness of the LORD in the land of the living. Wait for the LORD; be strong and take heart and wait for the LORD.

PSALM 27:13–14 NIV

I will never give up hope or stop praising You. All day long I will tell the wonderful things You do to save Your people.

PSALM 71:14—15 CEV

_____

God, You are so good, so faithful, so true.
Everything I have and everything I am comes from You.
With all my heart, I thank You, praise You,
and bless Your holy name.

YOU'VE BEEN CHOSEN

You are here today because, before the world began, God chose you. He chose to create you. He made sure of it. He loved you and wanted you to be with Him for all eternity. And He moved heaven and earth to make it possible. He sent His Son Jesus to remove every obstacle, every barrier, and to show you how to live in His light, His love. You have such a special place in His heart, a place no one else can fill. A purpose no one else can fill. You are loved. You are special. You are chosen.

You have been set apart as holy to the LORD your God,
and He has chosen you from all the nations of the earth to be
His own special treasure.

DEUTERONOMY 14:2 NLT

God knew what He was doing from the very beginning. He decided from
the outset to shape the lives of those who love Him along the same lines
as the life of His Son.... We see the original and intended shape of our
lives there in Him. After God made that decision of what His children
should be like, He followed it up by calling people by name. After He
called them by name, He set them on a solid basis with Himself. And
then, after getting them established, He stayed with them to the end,
gloriously completing what He had begun.

ROMANS 8:29–30 THE MESSAGE

I have chosen you and have not rejected you.

ISAIAH 41:9 NIV

Lord, thank You for choosing me. Thank You for loving me. Thank You for sending Jesus to bring me into this beautiful relationship with You. I love You!

STEP BY STEP

We are all on an epic journey, full of adventure, highs and lows, and twists and turns in the road. Sometimes it feels exciting, challenging, and rewarding. Sometimes it feels long and hard and lonely. But the truth is that we're never really alone. We have God to lead us and guide us. And we have friends and family to walk beside us—especially our spiritual family, our "brothers and sisters in Christ." It can take a little doing to navigate the differences in our personalities, backgrounds, and experiences. But by God's grace, we can come together, support, and strengthen one another. Step by step, we can keep each other company and keep each other courageous, as we make our way Home.

How good and pleasant it is when God's people live together in unity!
PSALM 133:1 NIV

You were all called to travel on the same road and in the same direction,
so stay together, both outwardly and inwardly.
EPHESIANS 4:4 THE MESSAGE

I will walk with you—I will be your God, and you will be My people.
LEVITICUS 26:12 CEV

I want you to get out there and walk—better yet, run!—
on the road God called you to travel.

EPHESIANS 4:1 THE MESSAGE

Father, thank You for the friends and family You've given me, for the people who walk this journey with me. Help me to encourage them even as they encourage me.

THE GOD WHO SEES

Hagar was a woman who'd been used and abused, despised, abandoned, and rejected. She didn't always respond to those wounds in the wisest or healthiest of ways. But God met her right where she was—in the midst of her hurt, anger, and despair. And He loved her. He loved this rebellious runaway slave girl. She may have felt invisible, but God told her that He knew her—He knew what she'd been through. He'd seen it all. He felt her pain. He understood. And He would help her. He would provide for her and protect her. He would lead her and guide her and give her a hope and a future.

This same God sees you, knows you, and loves you. He's waiting to meet you where you are today.

I will give thanks and praise You, O Lord my God, with all my heart; and will glorify Your name forevermore.

PSALM 86:12 AMP

He has looked [with loving care] on the humble state of His maidservant; for behold, from now on all generations will count me blessed and happy and favored by God!

LUKE 1:48 AMP

The LORD has been mindful of us; He will bless us.

PSALM 115:12 NASB

*She gave this name to the L*ORD *who spoke to her:*

"You are the God who sees me."

GENESIS 16:13 NIV

O Lord, how I love You! I praise Your holy Name.

How good it is to know that You are the God Who Sees Me

and I am the one known and loved by You.

WHAT'S YOUR PART?

Sometimes it's easy to see why others are important. Their gifts and talents are obvious. Their power, position, or influence is clear. Your own place might feel harder to find. But God says that you are just as crucial, just as significant, and just as important. You are a part of His family, His "Body," and He didn't make any extra or unnecessary parts. Yes, you have a vital role. The Body couldn't function without you. So don't waste time comparing yourself unfavorably to others or being envious or critical. Embrace the gifts and talents and responsibilities God has given you. And while you're at it, celebrate theirs too! Look for ways to work together for the benefit of everyone—and for His glory.

The human body has many parts, but the many parts make up one whole body. So it is with the body of Christ.

I CORINTHIANS 12:12 NLT

We are all parts of it, and it takes every one of us to make it complete, for we each have different work to do. So we belong to each other, and each needs all the others.

ROMANS 12:4—5 TLB

Make every effort to keep the oneness of the Spirit in the bond of peace [each individual working together to make the whole successful].

EPHESIANS 4:3 AMP

If each part of the body were the same part, there would be no body.
But truly God put the parts in the body as He wanted them. He made a
place for each one of them.

I CORINTHIANS 12:18 ICB

Lord Jesus, thank You for making me an important part of Your
Body. Help me to do my part to bring glory and honor to You.

JUST FORGIVEN

Have you made choices in your life that you still deeply regret? Are there things you struggle with today? In your heart of hearts, you long to do great things for God, but you wonder: how could He possibly use someone like me? Well, guess what? You're in good company! The Bible is full of mixed-up, messed-up people that God still used. Those men and women were all too human. They had serious character flaws. They made major mistakes. But God worked in them and through them to accomplish great and mighty things for His kingdom.

The Bible tells us it's in our weakness that God's power and strength is revealed. Through the cracks in our broken, messed-up lives, His light shines. People can see that it's not us but Jesus at work in us. We don't have to be perfect, just forgiven. Willing and available. Each and every day, by God's grace, ordinary people like us do extraordinary things for Him.

God chose the foolish things of the world to shame the wise; God chose the weak things of the world to shame the strong.

I CORINTHIANS 1:27 NIV

We now have this light shining in our hearts, but we ourselves are like fragile clay jars containing this great treasure. This makes it clear that our great power is from God, not from ourselves.

II CORINTHIANS 4:7 NLT

Therefore I will boast all the more gladly about my weaknesses, so that Christ's power may rest on me.

II CORINTHIANS 12:9 NIV

My dear friends, remember what you were when God chose you.

I CORINTHIANS 1:26 CEV

Jesus, thank You for Your steadfast love, forgiveness, mercy, and grace. Let my life today be a reflection of Your beauty and bring You great glory.

HIS MASTERPIECE

We are God's masterpiece, His greatest creation, His finest work. The Bible tells us that God was incredibly thoughtful, intentional, and deliberate about the process. It required great wisdom and skill; nothing about it was haphazard or accidental.

The result? Each of us is a true original—beautiful, one-of-a-kind, hand-crafted. We may not always feel so unique, so special, or so wonderful, but He says that we are. And when we listen, when we learn to believe it, we can resist the temptation to constantly measure and compare ourselves. We can let go of jealousy, insecurity, and competition. We can find joy, peace, contentment, and a sense of wonder in being His masterpiece.

What a wildly wonderful world, GOD! You made it all, with Wisdom at
Your side, made earth overflow with Your wonderful creations.

PSALM 104:24 THE MESSAGE

I praise You because You made me in an amazing and wonderful way.
What You have done is wonderful. I know this very well.

PSALM 139:14 ICB

With Your very own hands You formed me; now breathe Your wisdom
over me so I can understand You.

PSALM 119:73 THE MESSAGE

We are God's masterpiece. He has created us anew in Christ Jesus,
so we can do the good things He planned for us long ago.

EPHESIANS 2:10 NLT

God, help me to see myself the way You see me,

the beauty and creativity with which You crafted me,

Your masterpiece. And help me to see others the same way.

FOR SUCH A TIME

Long ago, a young Jewish girl named Esther won the most famous "beauty pageant" of all time and was chosen to be the bride of the king of Babylon. Later her cousin learned of a plot to annihilate the Jewish race and called on Esther to intervene with the king. At first, the queen was flabbergasted at the thought—at the risk involved in approaching her notoriously temperamental husband. It could literally cost her life. But God Himself had allowed Esther to become queen—had placed her in the palace—for this very moment. He had a plan to deliver His people and He wanted to use Esther to accomplish it.

God has a plan and a purpose for you too. At times you may feel overwhelmed. The task may seem too hard or the cost too high. But you've been blessed with the incredible privilege of being a "servant of the Most High." He has you where you are for a reason. He will give you all the courage and wisdom and strength you need. For you, too, are called—for such a time as this.

Peace I leave with you; My [perfect] peace I give to you.... Do not let your heart be troubled, nor let it be afraid. [Let My perfect peace calm you in every circumstance and give you courage and strength for every challenge.]

JOHN 14:27 AMP

"For I know the plans I have for you," declares the Lord, "plans to prosper you and not to harm you, plans to give you hope and a future."

JEREMIAH 29:11 NIV

Be courageous! Let us fight bravely for our people and the cities of our God.

II SAMUEL 10:12 NLT

Who knows whether you have not come to the kingdom for such a time as this?

ESTHER 4:14 ESV

God, I'm so honored that You have called me and chosen me to be part of Your glorious purposes, Your marvelous plans. Help me to be faithful to all that You ask.

PAYING IT FORWARD

Paul wrote a letter to Philemon, asking him to forgive a runaway servant and welcome him back with open arms, receiving him as a member of the family. That is exactly what he had become: a member of God's family, a sibling in the faith. Paul was confident that Philemon would honor this request, because Philemon was a man who knew that he himself had been forgiven; he himself had been set free. He knew he was blessed to be part of God's family.

When we know we have been blessed, we find no greater joy than passing on that blessing to others, finding ways to give back or pay it forward. Share the freedom.

It makes no difference whether you are a Jew or a Greek, a slave or
a freeman, a man or a woman, because in Jesus the Anointed, the
Liberating King, you are all one.
GALATIANS 3:28 VOICE

As you share your faith with others, I pray that they may come to know
all the blessings Christ has given us. My friend, your love has made me
happy and has greatly encouraged me. It has also cheered the hearts
of God's people.
PHILEMON 1:6–7 CEV

I do everything to spread the Good News and share in its blessings.
1 CORINTHIANS 9:23 NLT

You have been treated generously, so live generously.

MATTHEW 10:8 THE MESSAGE

Jesus, show me ways that I can express my love for You by blessing others as You have blessed me. Help me to give freely, cheerfully, and generously.

TAKE A BREATH

Breathe. It's going to be okay. It may feel as if you have a million impossible things to do, that you'll never get it all done, that no matter how hard you try, it's not enough. It may seem as if everyone (including you?) and everything around you is wildly spinning out of control, in desperate need of immediate intervention.

Just breathe. God's got this. You don't have to worry and stress. You don't have to plan and organize and prioritize and strategize in a full-on frenzy—especially when it only leaves you more anxious and overwhelmed than you were to start with. You don't need any of that. God is on the job. He's already working it out for His glory and your good. He's protecting and providing for you. Leading you and guiding you. Equipping you with everything—absolutely everything—you need. Don't borrow trouble. Be present in this moment. Be ready to receive.

Your Father knows exactly what you need even before you ask Him!
MATTHEW 6:8 NLT

Don't fret or worry. Instead of worrying, pray. Let petitions and praises shape your worries into prayers, letting God know your concerns. Before you know it, a sense of God's wholeness, everything coming together for good, will come and settle you down. It's wonderful what happens when Christ displaces worry at the center of your life.
PHILIPPIANS 4:6–7 THE MESSAGE

May the Lord watch over you and give you peace.
NUMBERS 6:26 ICB

Give your entire attention to what God is doing right now, and don't get worked up about what may or may not happen tomorrow. God will help you deal with whatever hard things come up when the time comes.

MATTHEW 6:34 THE MESSAGE

God, help me to let go of all the things that stress or worry me. Help me to trust You. Help me to rest in You. Help me to breathe.

BE A PEACEMAKER

Anyone can be a troublemaker. Anyone can gossip or grumble or complain. It's easy to provoke and irritate and agitate. But there's no real reward for that, and the consequences can be absolutely devastating—all around. God says there's a better way.

Be a peacemaker. Look for the good in others and help them do the same. Set a good example. Encourage those around you to be patient and kind, to show mercy and grace. When communication breaks down, prayerfully repair it with the goal of getting everyone on the same page. It's hard work, sometimes painful and painstaking work. Some of that work has to take place in our own heart first. But it's so worth it. The reward is significant; the impact can be eternal.

Be joyful. Grow to maturity. Encourage each other.
Live in harmony and peace.
II CORINTHIANS 13:11 NLT

Real wisdom, God's wisdom, begins with a holy life and is characterized
by getting along with others. It is gentle and reasonable, overflowing with
mercy and blessings, not hot one day and cold the next, not two-faced. You
can develop a healthy, robust community that lives right with God and
enjoy its results only if you do the hard work of getting along with each
other, treating each other with dignity and honor.
JAMES 3:17—18 THE MESSAGE

Those who are peacemakers will plant seeds of peace
and reap a harvest of righteousness.
JAMES 3:18 NLT

Blessed [spiritually calm with life-joy in God's favor]
are the makers and maintainers of peace.

MATTHEW 5:9 AMP

God, fill me with Your peace, and help me to bring
that peace into every relationship, every conflict, every situation
I find myself in today.

WINNING STRATEGY

Sometimes God tells His people to do things that don't seem to make a lot of sense. When they come to Him for problem solving, He gives them some pretty unusual strategies. For instance, He tells His people to march silently around and around a fortified city and then shout—to make the walls fall down. Or He says to send out a choir singing praises on the battlefield ahead of the army. Or wash seven times in a dirty river to be cured of leprosy. Or step right out into the middle of the Red Sea.

But He always has His reasons. And whenever God's people listen—whenever they obey—they always see Him work powerfully or miraculously. Let's keep that in mind as we ask Him for wisdom, guidance, or direction today.

This plan of Mine is not what you would work out, neither are My thoughts the same as yours! For just as the heavens are higher than the earth, so are My ways higher than yours, and My thoughts than yours.

ISAIAH 55:8—9 TLB

Trust in the LORD with all your heart; do not depend on your own understanding. Seek His will in all you do, and He will show you which path to take.

PROVERBS 3:5—6 NLT

Show me the right path, O LORD; point out the road for me to follow. Lead me by Your truth and teach me, for You are the God who saves me.

PSALM 25:4—5 NLT

Shout!—GOD has given you the city!

JOSHUA 6:16 THE MESSAGE

Lord, help me to hear You when You speak,

and give me the courage and faith to

do things Your way.

PRISONERS OF HOPE

Once we were prisoners of guilt and shame, of hopelessness and despair ... hurting and helpless, unable to save ourselves. But Jesus came to our rescue! He showed us mercy and grace. He brought us redemption, holiness, and healing. We live in this reality right now, in this life. There are moments—many moments—when we experience it. But we won't experience it fully and completely until we see Him face-to-face—until we're in heaven, our forever Home. So for now, we live as "prisoners of hope," facing life's challenges with His help, His strength, His grace and peace. Some days are harder than others. Some seasons are harder. But always, always, we live in glorious hope.

The LORD is my rock, my fortress, and my savior;
my God is my rock, in whom I find protection. He is my shield,
the power that saves me, and my place of safety.

PSALM 18:2 NLT

Return to your fortress, you prisoners of hope; even now I announce that
I will restore twice as much to you.

ZECHARIAH 9:12 NIV

As for those who grieve over Zion, God has sent Me to give them a
beautiful crown in exchange for ashes, to anoint them with gladness
instead of sorrow, to wrap them in victory, joy, and praise instead of
depression and sadness.

ISAIAH 61:3 VOICE

When you were stuck in your old sin-dead life, you were incapable of responding to God. God brought you alive—right along with Christ! Think of it! All sins forgiven, the slate wiped clean, that old arrest warrant canceled and nailed to Christ's cross.

COLOSSIANS 2:13–14 THE MESSAGE

Jesus, in Your great love, You have rescued me, saved me, set me free. Please let the reality of this sink into the deepest part of me—and let my heart sing!

HIS DELIGHT

God doesn't just love you—He likes you. In fact, He delights in you. You bring joy to His heart just by being you. He loves to hear your voice. He loves to see you smile. He loves spending time with you. God never thinks you're a burden or a bore. You are never an inconvenience or a disappointment to Him. No way. He loves your company. He looks for ways to connect with you. He finds all kinds of ways to show you how much He cares. When you're happy, He's rejoicing with you. When you're sad or angry or scared, He's listening. He's there to comfort you and strengthen you and help you. It's His pleasure.

As a groom is delighted with his bride,
so your God will delight in you.
ISAIAH 62:5 GNT

The LORD's delight is in those who fear Him,
those who put their hope in His unfailing love.
PSALM 147:11 NLT

The LORD takes delight in His people;
He crowns the humble with victory.
PSALM 149:4 NIV

He set me down in a safe place; He saved me to His delight; He took joy in me.

PSALM 18:19 VOICE

Lord, I can't even begin to understand how much You love me and how much You delight in me, but I'm so glad and grateful. Help me to love You and delight in You today.

BETTER TOGETHER

The unlikely friendship between Ruth and her mother-in-law, Naomi, is a beautiful example of what can happen when two people come together and find common ground, despite differences in age, background, culture, or personality. Two people decide to show up and stick around, to be there for each other, to love and support and encourage one another. It isn't always easy. Building and maintaining a lasting friendship can take hard work. It almost always requires extending grace and offering forgiveness, patience, and understanding. But this kind of friendship is so rewarding and such a gift—a powerful reminder that none of us have to make life's journey or face life's hardships alone. We have Jesus, and we have each other.

Friends love through all kinds of weather, and families stick together in all kinds of trouble.

PROVERBS 17:17 THE MESSAGE

Two people are better off than one, for they can help each other succeed. If one person falls, the other can reach out and help.

ECCLESIASTES 4:9–10 NLT

By yourself you're unprotected. With a friend you can face the worst.

ECCLESIASTES 4:12 THE MESSAGE

Wherever you go, I will go; wherever you live, I will live. Your people will be my people, and your God will be my God.

RUTH 1:16 NLT

Jesus, thank You for the gift of friendship and for the faithful friends You have given me. Help me to be a faithful friend to others.

HIDDEN BEAUTY

Sometimes we feel invisible—unseen. Sometimes we feel unknown, unappreciated, or unloved. Sometimes we wish that we could wish away the things that make us feel different or less than or not enough. But God says He sees us. He knows us. He loves us. He made us all the wonderful things we are, in all our glorious uniqueness. We are so precious to Him. We are more than enough. And He has big plans for us. If only we are willing to believe, willing to receive His love! Willing to let go of our insecurities and give up our complaints and comparisons. Let His love be the mirrored pool that reveals what He sees in us: that we are beautiful swans, not ugly ducklings.

Oh yes, You shaped me first inside, then out; You formed me in my mother's womb. I thank You, High God—You're breathtaking! Body and soul, I am marvelously made! I worship in adoration—what a creation! You know me inside and out, You know every bone in my body; You know exactly how I was made, bit by bit, how I was sculpted from nothing into something.

PSALM 139:13–15 THE MESSAGE

Like an open book, You watched me grow from conception to birth; all the stages of my life were spread out before You, the days of my life all prepared before I'd even lived one day.

PSALM 139:16 THE MESSAGE

My soul, bless the LORD, and all that is within me, bless His holy name.

PSALM 103:1 CSB

You have looked deep into my heart, LORD, and You know all about me.

PSALM 139:1 CEV

Lord, thank You for the life You have given me.

Help me to be a true reflection of Your love, Your beauty,

Your creativity, Your glory.

IMPORTANT WITNESS

Jesus has given you an important mission: He has called you to be His witness. A witness to the world, starting with your world: your family and friends, your community. He wants you to share with others what He has done for you, how He has worked in your heart and life, what you have seen and heard, what you have read in His Word.

It's a critical mission. There are so many lost and hurting people in this world, people who desperately need to know that they are loved, who desperately need to know that they are forgiven. You can be the one to bring them hope, bring them help, bring them to Jesus.

Go into all the world and preach the Good News to everyone.

MARK 16:15 NLT

You will receive power when the Holy Spirit comes upon you. And you will be My witnesses, telling people about Me everywhere.

ACTS 1:8 NLT

Give thanks to the LORD and proclaim His greatness. Let the whole world know what He has done.

PSALM 105:1 NLT

In the same way that You gave Me a mission in the world,
I give them a mission in the world.

JOHN 17:18 THE MESSAGE

Jesus, give me opportunities to be a witness for You today,

and give me the words to say. Help me share Your love and

Your light. Help me fulfill my mission with courage and grace.

#BLESSED

When we think of being #BLESSED—when we use that hashtag in our social posts—we're most often expressing gratitude or contentment. We're happy with our lives or the people in them; we're thankful for answers to prayer and evidence of God's loving care. We're celebrating good things, instead of complaining about bad things. And that's great!

But the Bible reminds us that these aren't the only times we're blessed and can give thanks. We're also blessed when everything goes wrong, when it feels as if we're under attack, when we aren't loved and appreciated or even respected. We're blessed when our faith brings us ridicule or rejection, when it costs us personally, physically, spiritually, or financially. Yes, because God is faithful, because He is always at work even in the worst that happens to us and because He can turn the worst into the best—we are truly blessed.

Don't run from tests and hardships, brothers and sisters. As difficult as they are, you will ultimately find joy in them; if you embrace them, your faith will blossom under pressure and teach you true patience as you endure. And true patience brought on by endurance will equip you to complete the long journey and cross the finish line—mature, complete, and wanting nothing.

JAMES 1:2 VOICE

You're not the only ones plunged into these hard times. It's the same with Christians all over the world. So keep a firm grip on the faith. The suffering won't last forever. It won't be long before this generous God who has great plans for us in Christ—eternal and glorious plans they are!— will have you put together and on your feet for good.

I PETER 5:9—10 THE MESSAGE

Blessed [comforted by inner peace and God's love] are those who are persecuted for doing that which is morally right, for theirs is the kingdom of heaven [both now and forever].

MATTHEW 5:10 AMP

Lord Jesus, help me to count myself blessed and to bring glory to You even on hard days and during hard times. Keep me faithful to You, just as You are faithful to me.

NO WALLFLOWERS

We're not hugging the wall, hiding in the corner, waiting for someone to notice us—hoping someone will notice us. Not anymore. We're not wishing we were someone else, feeling intimidated, insecure, less-than by comparison. No way! God has loved us. He has chosen us. He has created us to be bold, beautiful reflections of His glory, each in our own unique and special way. It's true that we have our faults and flaws and our brokenness. But Jesus covers it all. He forgives, heals, and restores. In Him we are strong. In Him we are free: free to take center stage in our own story and be all He means for us to be.

*Because of Christ and our faith in Him, we can now come boldly and
confidently into God's presence.*

EPHESIANS 3:12 NLT

My heart rejoices in the LORD! The LORD has made me strong.

I SAMUEL 2:1 NLT

*My heart is confident in You, O God; my heart is confident.
No wonder I can sing Your praises!*

PSALM 57:7 NLT

Since this new way gives us such confidence, we can be very bold.

II CORINTHIANS 3:12 NLT

Lord Jesus, help me to live boldly and courageously, knowing how much You love me. You're rooting for me and cheering me on to victory!

A PURPOSEFUL LIFE

Anna is an elderly widow mentioned in the Gospel of Luke. She lived a life fully dedicated to God—a life of prayer and worship. As the years passed, she found even greater purpose in pointing others to Jesus, telling them the news of the coming Savior, even though she didn't know when he would appear. She chose to tell them what she had seen and heard and what she had learned. She had a lifetime of wisdom, a lifetime of experience. She was a firsthand witness, not only to the coming of the Messiah (the birth of Jesus) but to God's faithfulness for generations. Her ministry was even more meaningful, more powerful, more relevant in her eighties than it had ever been because she was faithful to her purpose, her calling. She simply pointed others to Jesus. May that be said of us all.

My mouth will tell of Your righteous deeds, of Your saving acts all day long—though I know not how to relate them all. I will come and proclaim Your mighty acts, Sovereign LORD; I will proclaim Your righteous deeds, Yours alone. Since my youth, God, You have taught me, and to this day I declare Your marvelous deeds. Even when I am old and gray, do not forsake me, my God, till I declare Your power to the next generation, Your mighty acts to all who are to come.

PSALM 71:15–18 NIV

It is for this that we labor and strive [often called to account], because we have fixed our [confident] hope on the living God, who is the Savior of all people, especially of those who believe [in Him, recognize Him as the Son of God, and accept Him as Savior and Lord].

I TIMOTHY 4:10 AMP

She began speaking out thanks to God, and she continued spreading the word about Jesus to all those who shared her hope for the rescue of Jerusalem.

LUKE 2:38 VOICE

Lord Jesus, in all I say and do,

help me faithfully point others to You.

SAFELY HELD

Do you ever feel like Alice in Wonderland—as if you've somehow tumbled down a rabbit hole and everything in your world is now upside down or backward or jumbled? Nothing seems right. Nothing makes sense. You're falling ... falling ... falling. When will it end? How will it end?

Maybe you think it's your own fault, the result of choices you've made. Or maybe what's happening to you is the result of a choice made by someone else. Either way, it's dark and scary and disorienting.

But no matter how it feels, you aren't helplessly free-falling through one disaster after another, spinning wildly out of control. No, through it all, you are being held—gently but firmly—by God. He is in control. And He will never let anything separate you from His love. Nothing and no one can ever take you out of His hands.

He [God] has said, "I WILL NEVER *[under any circumstances]* DESERT
YOU *[nor give you up nor leave you without support, nor will I in any
degree leave you helpless],* NOR WILL I FORSAKE *or* LET YOU DOWN *or*
RELAX MY HOLD ON YOU *[assuredly not]!*

HEBREWS 13:5 AMP

*Offer praise to God our Savior because of our Lord Jesus Christ! Only
God can keep you from falling and make you pure and joyful in His
glorious presence. Before time began and now and forevermore, God is
worthy of glory, honor, power, and authority. Amen.*

JUDE 1:24—25 CEV

I give them a life that is unceasing, and death will not have the last word.
Nothing or no one can steal them from My hand.

JOHN 10:28 VOICE

Father God, hold me close—so close that I can hear Your

heartbeat. Keep me safe and help me rest in Your love.

JOYFUL, JOYFUL

You can do this! You can find joy. You can choose joy. You have reason to rejoice—actually, dozens and dozens of reasons, no matter what's going on in your world or how it's treating you. You have a heavenly Father who loves you so much, cares so deeply about everything that happens to you, and has the power to work in and through all of it for His glory and your good.

He has promised that there is so much joy ahead. He has many great things in store for you. Some of it will have to wait until this life is through, but it will keep. And in the meantime, He offers you not only His grace and peace, but His joy. He shares with you His own deep, living, lasting joy—joy that will equip you and empower you to take on life's challenges to emerge victorious. Let His joy be your strength today.

We pray that you'll have the strength to stick it out over the long haul—not the grim strength of gritting your teeth but the glory-strength God gives. It is strength that endures the unendurable and spills over into joy, thanking the Father who makes us strong enough to take part in everything bright and beautiful that He has for us.

COLOSSIANS 1:11 THE MESSAGE

The LORD is my strength and shield. I trust Him with all my heart. He helps me, and my heart is filled with joy. I burst out in songs of thanksgiving.

PSALM 28:7 NLT

Rejoice in the Lord always [delight, take pleasure in Him]; again I will say, rejoice!

PHILIPPIANS 4:4 AMP

The joy of the LORD is your strength!

NEHEMIAH 8:10 NLT

Lord Jesus, fill me with Your deep joy. Help me to look for it, find it, receive it, and choose it again and again today.

HANDS AND FEET

Teresa of Avila once said, "Christ has no body on earth but yours, no hands but yours, no feet but yours. Yours are the eyes through which Christ's compassion for the world is to look out; yours are the feet with which He is to go about doing good; and yours are the hands with which He is to bless us now."

There are so many hurting people in this world. Some of them are in your own family, church, workplace, neighborhood, or community. By God's grace and in His strength, you can help them. You can go to them. You can hold them. You can love them and comfort them, strengthen them and encourage them. You can remind them how much they mean to God and how special they are to Him. You can be His hands and feet today.

Serve each other with love.

GALATIANS 5:13 ICB

Speak encouraging words to one another. Build up hope so you'll all be together in this, no one left out, no one left behind. I know you're already doing this; just keep on doing it.

I THESSALONIANS 5:11 THE MESSAGE

We will lovingly follow the truth at all times—speaking truly, dealing truly, living truly—and so become more and more in every way like Christ who is the Head of His body, the Church. Under His direction, the whole body is fitted together perfectly, and each part in its own special way helps the other parts, so that the whole body is healthy and growing and full of love.

EPHESIANS 4:15 TLB

Comfort each other and give each other strength, just as you are doing now.

I THESSALONIANS 5:11 ICB

Jesus, show me the hurting people You want me to serve in Your name. Help me to know what to say and what to do so that they feel Your presence and love.

SAFELY HOME

Jesus is the Good Shepherd. Your Good Shepherd. You can trust Him to safely lead. He will provide for you and protect you, strengthen you and guide you through the mountains and the valleys. And when you get distracted or discouraged, when you wander off the path, when you get lost, He won't leave you behind, leave you to figure it out, or leave you to find your own way home. He will come looking for you. He will find you. You are that precious, that special, that important to Him. You are His. If you are struggling or stumbling, if you are hurting, He will pick you up and carry you. Nothing will keep Him from bringing you safely home.

I myself am the shepherd. I'm going looking for them. As shepherds go after their flocks when they get scattered, I'm going after my sheep. I'll rescue them from all the places they've been scattered.

EZEKIEL 34:11 THE MESSAGE

I will look for those that are lost, bring back those that wander off, bandage those that are hurt, and heal those that are sick.

EZEKIEL 34:16 GNT

I will seek my lost ones, those who strayed away, and bring them safely home again.

EZEKIEL 34:16 TLB

The LORD is my Shepherd.... He lets me rest in green meadows; He leads me beside peaceful streams. He renews my strength. He guides me along right paths, bringing honor to His name.

PSALM 23:1–3 NLT

Jesus, Shepherd of my heart, hold me close. Lead me and guide me and stay beside me, all the long journey.

A GLORIOUS FUTURE

God's people grieved that His temple lay in ruins, first destroyed by enemies and then neglected—left damaged, only to decay. But as they began the monumental, almost impossible task of rebuilding, God spoke words of hope to their hearts. One day His temple would be completely restored, and this "new temple" would be far more beautiful, more glorious, more magnificent than they could imagine. And He didn't mean the building.

He was looking ahead to Jesus—and to us. Scripture tells us that we are now God's temple, His dwelling place. He makes His home in our hearts. We worship Him in all that we do and with all that we are. And when any part of us struggles or suffers or starts falling apart—heart, soul, body, or mind—it only points us to another future glory: that day when every part of us will be fully redeemed and restored, made whole and complete in Him, in heaven, forever and ever!

For you who fear My Name, the Sun of Righteousness will rise
with healing in His wings.

MALACHI 4:2 NLT

On that day you will be glad, even if you have to go through
many hard trials for a while.

I PETER 1:6 CEV

Surely you have a wonderful future ahead of you. There is hope for you yet!

PROVERBS 23:18 TLB

This Temple is going to end up far better than it started out, a glorious beginning but an even more glorious finish: a place in which I will hand out wholeness and holiness.

HAGGAI 2:9 THE MESSAGE

God, thank You for giving me such a glorious hope,

such a wonderful, beautiful future to look forward to!

Help me to live in the light of that hope today.

GROWING DEEP

How can we hold onto hope in seasons of loss, grief, and pain? How can we stand strong when it feels as if we've lost the ground beneath our feet? How can we not just survive but thrive, even in hard times? By choosing to trust in God's unfailing love for us. Scripture tells us that this love is so deep and so high and so wide, it can't be measured. It's a love that not only truly wants what's best for us, but actually *knows* what's best for us—much better than we know ourselves. This is the love that created us, the love that sustains us, the love that says it will not let us go. This love promises that nothing we experience—no hardship, heartache, or pain—is ever wasted. There is nothing in our lives that can't somehow be redeemed or restored or renewed. This love can transform anything! Better days are coming; they really are. But we can flourish even on our worst days, nourished by the deep, deep love of God.

Look, I am making everything new!

REVELATION 21:5 NLT

I will give you back what you lost....
And you will praise the LORD your God.

JOEL 2:25—26 NLT

I'll plant your roots deep in the land I have given you,
and you won't ever be uprooted again.

AMOS 9:15 CEV

I am like an olive tree flourishing in the house of God;
I trust in God's unfailing love for ever and ever.

PSALM 52:8 NIV

Dear Jesus, help me to grasp—or at least get a sense of—
the depth of Your love for me. Let it fill me with hope and lift
me above my circumstances today.

HE NEVER SLEEPS

Sometimes we feel small, alone, and scared. It seems like the whole world is against us, and we don't know what to do or where to go or who to turn to. But God says that we are not alone. We are never alone. He is always, always with us. And He is always ready to help us. Turn to Him. He will support and strengthen us. He will lead us and guide us. He will protect and defend us. He will be our safe place—He will "hide" us. At night, we can sleep—really sleep, sleep well because He's keeping watch. And He never sleeps.

Every word of God proves true. He is a shield to all
who come to Him for protection.
PROVERBS 30:5 NLT

He will cover you with His wings; you will be safe in His care;
His faithfulness will protect and defend you.
PSALM 91:4 GNT

God guards you from every evil, He guards your very life. He guards
you when you leave and when you return, He guards you now,
He guards you always.
PSALM 121:7—8 THE MESSAGE

He will never let me stumble, slip, or fall.
For He is always watching, never sleeping.

PSALM 121:3–4 TLB

Thank You, God, for watching over me, protecting me,

and providing for me. Help me rest in the love You have for me.

PRESS ON

No more hiding or hanging your head in shame. No more reliving all the failures and mistakes of the past. No more hesitating. No more looking back. No more false start or staggering and stumbling over the same old obstacles time and time again. Shake it off. God's got this! His grace continually covers it all. Now it's time to run. Run headlong into the next adventure, the new season. Run with focus and determination. Run with passion and perseverance. Run to win. We can do this—we really can—because we are loved. We are forgiven. We are free.

Therefore, since we are surrounded by such a huge crowd of witnesses to the life of faith, let us strip off every weight that slows us down, especially the sin that so easily trips us up. And let us run with endurance the race God has set before us.

HEBREWS 12:1 NLT

Throw off your old sinful nature and your former way of life, which is corrupted by lust and deception. Instead, let the Spirit renew your thoughts and attitudes. Put on your new nature, created to be like God— truly righteous and holy.

EPHESIANS 4:22—24 NLT

Take on an entirely new way of life—a God-fashioned life, a life renewed from the inside and working itself into your conduct as God accurately reproduces His character in you.

EPHESIANS 4:24 THE MESSAGE

If we [freely] admit that we have sinned and confess our sins, He is faithful
and just [true to His own nature and promises], and will forgive our sins
and cleanse us continually from all unrighteousness [our wrongdoing,
everything not in conformity with His will and purpose].

I JOHN 1:9 AMP

Father, give me the courage and strength and grace to run this

race. You have made me new and I am victorious in You!

A BENEDICTION

Someone once said, "Yesterday is history; tomorrow is a mystery. Today is a gift—that's why it is called the present." The Bible reminds us that God holds it all—past, present, and future—in His hands. He holds us in His hands. We are intimately known and deeply loved by Him. We are forgiven. We are so special, so important to Him. He has great plans and purposes for us, and He equips us with everything we need to accomplish these things. And we are never alone. He leads us and guides us every step of the way. He blesses our lives and fills our hearts with hope.

God has been good to us in the past. He has proved Himself faithful time and time again. With courage and confidence, we can face whatever comes our way today, looking forward to a glorious future forever and ever with Him.

Watch for His return; expect the blessed hope we all will share when our great God and Savior, Jesus the Anointed, appears again.

TITUS 2:13 VOICE

My friends, that's why you must remain faithful and follow closely what we taught you in person and by our letters.

II THESSALONIANS 2:15 CEV

Now may our Lord Jesus Christ Himself and God our Father, who has loved us and given us everlasting comfort and encouragement and the good [well-founded] hope [of salvation] by His grace, comfort and encourage and strengthen your hearts [keeping them steadfast and on course] in every good work and word.

II THESSALONIANS 2:16—17 AMP

May the God of hope fill you with all joy and peace as you trust in Him,
so that you may overflow with hope by the power of the Holy Spirit.

ROMANS 15:13 NIV

_____
_____
_____
_____
_____
_____
_____
_____
_____
_____
_____
_____
_____
_____
_____
_____

Jesus, how I long to see You face-to-face and live happily ever after with You! Until then, fill me with hope and encouragement for each new day.

Want More? Check out

The DaySpring Hope and Encouragement Bible,

and our *Prayers to Share: 100 Pass-Along Notes*

of Hope & Encouragement.

PRAYERS TO SHARE

—— 100 ——

PASS-ALONG NOTES

FOR

*Hope &
Encouragement*

*Available at DaySpring.com
and several retailers in your area.*